COOK'S
PROGRESS

COOK'S PROGRESS

Simone Sekers

With Drawings By Ian Beck
Compton Press

© Simone Sekers 1979

First published by The Compton Press Ltd 1979

ISBN 0 900193 70 0

Designed by Humphrey Stone
and printed by The Compton Press Ltd
The Old Brewery, Tisbury, Wilts

To my patient family and friends,
with thanks

Contents

Introduction

I am lucky enough to be one of a generation which mercifully knows little or nothing about the kind of bad English cooking which prevailed between the two wars. It must have been a depressing time; the age of Brown Windsor soup, grey lumps of gristle called Irish Stew, boiled cod and blancmange. There were outposts of civilization where traditional English cooks reigned supreme, producing treacle pudding and devilled kidneys and jugged hare; but, on the whole the outlook was grim, until the publication of Elizabeth David's first book in 1950. Slowly but surely the outlook brightened; provincial shops began to stock garlic and olive oil; then, one day, the last cloud rolled away and *ratatouille* emerged on enlightened tables up and down the country.

At about this time I was thrown in at the deep end, being sent, with a brand-new husband, to Lyons, to start my married life with schoolroom French and Mrs David as my only guide to the mysteries of *la cuisine française*. Her recipes were my saving; I had to feed not only my husband, but also, sometimes, his sister's French in-laws, cooking on a two-ring cooker in a bed-sitter hung about with plastic geraniums. Armed with the title of a dish like *épaule d'agneau boulangère* (which sounded economical because it contained potatoes), I was able to buy what I wanted from helpful market stall-holders. They gave me advice about the right sort of potatoes, the correct herbs, even how much garlic to add – not *too* much in a salad, *never* too much in a *bouillabaisse* – and, above all, to be uncompromising about the quality of food. It all began to fall into place. We ate meals with French families which were triumphs of unpretentious perfection; a plate of leeks *à la grecque* followed by lamb cooked slowly with haricot beans, a salad, then one or two local cheeses in perfect condition, ending with a pyramid of mahogany-coloured pears baked gently in red wine while the lamb cooked in the same oven. This was *la cuisine soignée*; it was their way of life, and I decided it would become mine.

This book is about that school of cooking, although it is not exclusively about French food. I have tried to include recipes from Italy, Spain, Greece and the Middle East, but have placed particular emphasis on good English recipes, which retired into oblivion during the Dark Age of British food, and which writers like Jane Grigson and Sheila Hutchinson have done so much to revive in the past few years.

With care and planning *la cuisine soignée* can be achieved by a natural progression from day to day, of good freshly prepared food from larder to table rather than a frenzied scrabble in the freezer at the last minute. Freezers are certainly useful, but like stock cubes, are best used in moderation.

SIMONE SEKERS 1978

The Well-Stocked Larder

The Well-Stocked Larder

One of the most time-consuming aspects of cooking is shopping; if you have to go out and buy all the ingredients every time you want to produce a special dish, then the special dishes naturally become rarer. This larder list is obviously only a rough guide, based on personal experience of things I find useful.

Tins

Italian tomatoes are indispensable for soups, stews and sauces during the major part of the year when fresh tomatoes are tasteless and expensive.

Baked beans, provided your family likes them.

Belgian or French *petits pois* and *flageolets* are much nicer than frozen ones, and more convenient. The *flageolets* are particularly good enlivened with chopped parsley and garlic as a quick meal with lamb chops, or even bacon rashers.

Tuna is always useful, particularly in the summer for Italian dishes like *vitello tonnato* (page 86), and *tonno e fagioli* (page 56). Kedgeree made with tuna is a good winter Saturday lunch which children seem to love.

Anchovies: for sauces, fish dishes, savoury butters, or as part of a first course.

Black cherries (as fresh ones never seem to get cheap enough to do anything with). Polish bottled varieties are good, inexpensive, and make lovely puddings.

Pulses and Pasta

Two vital items, particularly if you regularly run out of potatoes, or need to stretch meals.

Chick peas, green lentils, split peas and haricot beans are usually available in large supermarkets, but you may have to go to a health food shop to find the lentils. On the whole, the longer you store them, the more cooking they will need, so buy them in fairly small quantities.

The same can be said for pasta – it does not keep indefinitely. Supermarkets' 'own' brands are often as good, and far cheaper, than the imported brands from delicatessens – both Tesco and Sainsbury have good pasta. I like to keep stocks of green lasagne, egg noodles and ordinary spaghetti.

Rice and other cereals

I prefer to keep two or three different kinds of rice: cheap long-grain rice bought in bulk for ordinary savoury dishes; Basmati rice (from Indian grocers and some health stores) for special dishes, especially Middle Eastern pilaffs, because of its delicious flavour; and Italian rice for real *risottos* (Tesco and Sainsbury's often sell it under the name 'Easy-Cook'; the grains are shorter, fatter and more transparent than ordinary long-grain rice). Brown rice is less useful, as not everyone likes its aggressively 'healthy' texture, and it does take much longer to cook.

Small quantities of medium oatmeal and buckwheat are handy to have for coating herrings, making parkin, or, in the case of buckwheat, for stuffings, or as an alternative to rice (see page 109).

Baking ingredients

If your family likes cakes, puddings, pastry and home-made bread, some, if not all, of these items should be in the larder:

Wholemeal and strong plain flour, and dried yeast (easier to store for emergencies than fresh yeast).

Plain flour and baking powder. This is particularly important if you are short of space because you won't need to store self-raising flour as well.

Bicarbonate of soda.

Brown sugar (moist is better than demerara).

Black treacle and golden syrup.

Caster and icing sugar.

Dried fruit; candied peel; nuts (small packets of unblanched almonds, hazelnuts, and walnuts, kept in a screw-top jar).

Flavourings: good quality almond and vanilla essence.

Cocoa and/or good cooking chocolate: Bournville and Chocolat Menier are both good.

Spices: cloves; cinnamon; nutmeg; ginger, both whole and powdered.

Seasonings and other condiments

Mustard: mustard powder for flavouring sauces; Meaux mustard (one of the English versions, like Urchfont or Colman's, if you cannot find the French one in its lovely, useful, stoneware jar); Dijon mustard; and Colman's American mustard for children's hot-dogs and hamburgers.

Peppercorns. I buy these in bulk, in a large airtight tin, rather than in fancy packs. They seem to keep very well. Green peppercorns in brine are now widely available and are delicious with game, fish and pork.

Juniper berries: for *pâtés*, game and veal.

Coriander seeds. I keep mine in their own peppergrinder by the cooker. They can often be bought more cheaply from chemists than from grocers, and this goes for most spices. Store them away from light and air in small tins. Wooden spice towers or black tin spice boxes can still be found in junk-shops, and are far better for storing spices than pretty glass jars.

Vanilla pods: for flavouring custards, etc. They usually come in their own stoppered glass tube. Always keep one or two, cut in half, in a jar of caster sugar, topping it up as you use it, for sprinkling on pancakes or for flavouring cakes.

Salt. I keep Maldon salt crystals for the table, and used crushed block salt for cooking.

Indian spices: turmeric; cumin; caraway, etc. Buy them in small tins from an Indian grocer, if possible.

Herbs are always best fresh, of course, but bayleaves, basil, oregano, thyme and rosemary are all good dried. Again, like spices, they should be stored in the dark.

Anchovy essence is useful for flavouring fish dishes and savoury butters.

Mushroom ketchup and Worcester sauce are both good for adding extra flavour to soups and stews.

Capers and gherkins, or pickled cucumbers, are useful for *vinaigrette* based sauces, as well as serving with *hors d'oeuvres*.

Vinegar: cider and/or both red and white wine vinegar (not malt vinegar, except for fish and chips).

Oil. Buy the best olive oil you can afford, and in the largest quantity you can afford to, as it is always cheaper like that. Sunflower oil is slightly cheaper, and some people prefer its milder flavour when it comes to making mayonnaise. Crisp n'Dry oil is excellent for deep-frying, as it can be re-used many times, and has little or no flavour.

Tomato purée. Always keep a tube in the fridge.

Stock cubes and powder. Useful in moderation, or everything will taste as if it has come out of a packet.

Breadcrumbs. Make your own by browning cubes of white bread in a low oven when you have it on for some other reason. Whiz them in the blender, or crush them between two sheets of grease-proof paper with a rolling pin, then store them in a screw-top jar. Fresh white breadcrumbs are very useful to have in the freezer, if you have one, for making lighter dumplings and suet crusts, as well as forcemeat balls; they do not need to be defrosted first.

Basic fresh foods

Eggs are the most obvious items to keep in the larder (not in the fridge). A wall-hung egg rack is good if you are short of space.

Bacon. Home-cured is nicest, and streaky the most useful for general cooking purposes.

Cheese. A whole Cheddar is one of the best larder items I know, particularly in the school holidays. You can buy them by post from L. & M. Montgomery, Manor Farm, South Cadbury, Somerset; the postage is exorbitant, but the marvellous quality of the cheese more than makes up for this. Parmesan is essential for Italian dishes, and if you can't buy it by the piece, a well-packed Italian brand is best.

Lemons and oranges: for drinks, sweet dishes and general good health. A plastic lemon kept in the fridge is convenient, but very much second-best.

Garlic. Feel it carefully before buying, to make sure it is good and solid. A small wire garlic basket, hung on a hook near the cooker is the best way to store it.

Onions. Store them as you would garlic, with plenty of air circulating round; a string shopping-bag is good. Dried onions are useful and surprisingly good.

Potatoes. If you eat a lot and have the space, buy a sack or two of good quality ones (King Edwards are the best all-rounders) in the autumn, to save carting heavy bags home twice a week.

Parsley. Dried parsley is quite useless, so try growing your own, either in the garden or in a parsley-pot on the window-sill. It can be stored in a polythene box in the fridge for a week or so.

Cream. An essential luxury. Look for the 'sell-by' date when you buy it, and you might be able to keep it for up to a week in the fridge.

Butter. I always buy the cheapest on offer, but like to have a supply of unsalted butter for sweet dishes. Soft margarine makes cake-making much easier.

Useful luxuries

Cooking wine. Buy the cheapest wine you can find, one bottle each of red and white. Dry cider is also useful, and a half-bottle of madeira, port or sweet sherry will make all the difference to syrups and sauces. A quarter-bottle of cheap grape brandy is a worthwhile standby, particularly at Christmas.

Some form of sausage or ham hanging in the larder is a very good investment. The price of a whole, really good, French or Italian garlic sausage or smoked ham may make you nervous initially, but it will be so much better than anything you can buy ready sliced that you will find it worthwhile. French *jambons fumés* are almost as good as the Italian ones, and much cheaper, while Italian salami are usually cheaper than French garlic sausage. Store them by wrapping in an old pillowcase and hanging them in an airy place.

Preserving
Without
Freezing

Preserving Without Freezing

The following methods are all for preserving food by traditional means – methods which have all but disappeared in the face of modern 'convenience' foods. In fact, these *are* convenience foods – to be made when ingredients are cheap and plentiful, and to have on hand for instant use, with no defrosting problems.

THE BRINE-JAR

This is a way of keeping meat for long periods while at the same time improving its flavour and texture. You will need a container, with a lid, which will hold about 1 gallon of brine; earthenware is too porous, plastic becomes dingy – I prefer stoneware. The important thing is to be able to sterilize it with boiling water and soda. The brine itself is made as follows:

7 pints water	2 bayleaves
1½-2 lb cooking or block salt	6 juniper berries
2 oz saltpetre	10 peppercorns
¾ lb brown sugar	½ a nutmeg
1 sprig rosemary	6 cloves
2 sprigs thyme	1 teasp coriander seeds

Sea-salt is often recommended for making brine, but I prefer the blocks of Cheshire salt, available from a good grocer or health food shop. Saltpetre is available from dispensing chemists. Buy only a little at a time as it absorbs moisture very easily and is therefore difficult to store. It is necessary, as it gives the meat a healthy pink colour, without which it would be grey and unappetizing. It does harden the meat, however, so you need to add sugar to counteract this, as well as to improve the flavour. Tie the herbs and spices securely into a clean, old, handkerchief, and crush this bundle gently to bruise (not pulverize) the contents. Put everything into a large saucepan and bring slowly to the boil, pressing the spice bundle with a wooden spoon every so often. Allow the brine to boil for a minute or two before withdrawing it from the heat. Cover the pan and allow the brine to get quite cold. Meanwhile, find a plate which will fit neatly inside your brine-jar, and a weight (a large scrubbed stone will do very well). The weight and plate will keep the meat submerged. Pour the cold brine through a sieve into the container. Put in your meat (*see below*), fit the plate on top of the meat, then the weight and finally the lid, which can be improvised if the jar does not have its own – a piece of wood, or plastic sheeting, or even a clean tea-cloth will do. Store the jar in a cool place; a garage or garden-shed if you have no larder.

Now for suitable meats and their brine-timing. My own favourite is pork, and particularly belly pork. Ask the butcher to remove the bones, then put it into the brine. Five days to a week is the minimum time for, say, a 3 lb piece, but you can store it for at least two months.

A leg of pork can be kept in brine for a month, then cooked like a ham; it will have a deliciously mild flavour and is excellent as a Christmas dish.

Joints of pork for roasting will benefit from a few hours in brine; it will make them more digestible as well as improving the flavour.

Pure pork sausages, *i.e.* made entirely of pork or with a *very* small proportion of cereal (from Marks & Spencer, if you do not have a butcher who makes the type known as 'Cumberland' sausage), can be put into brine for 2-3 days, then poached like a boiling sausage and served with lentils or a potato salad. The brine gives them extra flavour.

Calves', lambs' and pigs' tongues will all need about a week and you can prepare an ox-tongue yourself by leaving it in brine for a fortnight. That way you can be sure it will not be too salty, without having to take your butcher's word for it.

Silverside of beef is the classic joint for salting and a 3 lb piece will need about 10 days. Brisket is also very good; the brine will break down the tough fibres and make this otherwise fatty joint delicious.

The above are the best pieces of meat for salting, but you can always experiment. Try lamb, for example. All meat can be kept for several weeks in brine. Do not be dismayed by the sinister blanket of mould which will form on the surface. It can be lifted off, and, underneath, the meat will be perfectly good. The longer you leave meat in brine, however, the more likely it is to need soaking before cooking, to get rid of excess salt. If you are removing a sizable joint from the brine, it is just as well to reboil the brine with another pound of salt, as you will be removing some of the salt with the meat. Allow it to get quite cold before returning it to the jar.

DRY SALTING

This is a more refined version of the brine-jar method, in which spiced salt is rubbed into the meat daily over a period of time. I give details of its various aspects under separate headings in later chapters, like the recipe for spiced duck on page 111 but I would also include the marinade method, which is a short-term way of preserving meat and at the same time altering its flavour (*see* recipes on pages 112, 114).

POTTED MEATS

Potting is the best way of preserving cooked meat, and is a better way of storing *pâtés* than freezing them. Leave the *pâté* in the dish in which it was cooked and seal it with about ¾" lard, melted and poured over the top; wrap the whole dish, lid and all, in foil, then store it for up to three weeks in the bottom of the fridge. The flavours will have a chance to blend and mellow, the lard will be useful for frying potatoes, you will retain the delicious jelly surrounding the *pâté* (which the deep-freezing process seems to dissolve), and the texture will be all the better for not having expanded and contracted in the freezing and the defrosting.

Rillettes (*see* page 59 for the recipe)

These are cheap and easy to make and are excellent as an *hors d'oeuvres*. *Rillettes* too, keep well when sealed with lard. I have kept them for up to a month, at the end of which they were noticeably better than if they had been eaten the moment they were made.

Confits

The best known is probably *confit d'oie*, the preserved goose which is an important part of a good Toulouse *cassoulet*. With goose at its present price this may not be feasible, but duck, rabbit, chicken and pork are all good preserved in this way. I will give the recipe here, as it is a general one.

Confits

First, cut your meat into portions which will fit easily into the largest size of Kilner jar, then rub it with the following mixture:

1 lb crushed block salt	6 crushed juniper berries
2 crumbled bayleaves	6 crushed black peppercorns
1 sprig crumbled dried thyme	Pinch saltpetre

Leave the meat to stand overnight. Next day, wipe the pieces of meat and put them into a large casserole with enough melted lard to cover the meat completely. Put on a well-fitting lid and cook in a low oven (about 300°F) until the meat is tender (the saltpetre will make it look pink; do not overcook because of this. Rabbit and chicken will take about 1 hour, pork and duck just under 2). Drain the meat in a colander and leave the lard in which it cooked to harden. Pour an inch of fresh melted lard into the scrupulously clean jars, put in the pieces of meat (keeping different varieties separate), and then top up to the brim, with more melted lard. You can re-use the cooking lard once it has solidified enough to lift it out of its pan, leaving behind the meat juices, which will turn the preserved meat sour if included. Fit greaseproof paper disks over the jars before putting on the proper Kilner lids; label each jar clearly with the type of meat and its date of preservation – it will keep at least 6 months in a cool larder. To use the meat, stand the jar in a warm oven until the lard melts enough to be able to lift out the meat with a fork. The meat can then be reheated under the grill and served with potato purée and a sharp sauce, or it can be served cold, with pickles or chutneys, but best of all, add it to a version of the *cassoulet*, like that on page 96.

POTTED FISH

Some sort of salt or pickled fish is often part of a mixed *hors d'oeuvres;* anchovies and sardines are the two most familiar, easily available in tinned form. It is easy to pickle your own fish, and members of the herring family are the best subjects. There are several recipes for doing this in the chapter on first courses (*see* pages 56, 57, 58).

So much for preserved meat and fish, and for the variety they can provide in everyday meals. The small trouble taken is worth it, and while the preparation is sometimes lengthy, you can almost always be doing something else during that preparation – you don't need to stand over cooling brine, or *confits* slowly cooking in the oven.

Next come the more ordinary aspects of home preservation; pickles, chutneys, jams, jellies and bottled fruit. One of the nicest and most satisfying sights in the larder is a shelf or two of glowing jars of fruit. The preparation of fruit for bottling and freezing is very much the same, but the convenience of bottled fruit is obvious, as it is instantly ready to eat. Recipes will be found on pages 157, 158, 159.

I have not included such things as preserved eggs and salted runner beans, because they are somehow reminiscent of a siege economy. It is possible to buy eggs and green vegetables all the year round, thanks to modern methods of agriculture. However distasteful these methods may sometimes seem, they are not nearly as bad as eggs preserved in waterglass and platefuls of very salty beans.

Kitchen Equipment

Kitchen Equipment

Basic equipment – pans, knives, chopping blocks – should all be of the best quality you can afford, to give a lifetime of use.

Choose heavy saucepans with well-fitting lids and heat-proof handles; make sure really large pans have an additional hand-hold opposite the handle, to use when the saucepan is full and heavy. Non-stick linings *can* be useful, if you are prepared to take care of them; personally, I prefer to have a saucepan or frying-pan I can scrape with a metal spoon, or scour with wire-wool if I want to, rather than have the bother of remembering not to do those things. A *bain-marie* is not essential – a basin which fits neatly into an ordinary saucepan will do almost as well – but it does help if you make a lot of sauces not to have to fumble around for the right basin and the right pan, which you may be using for something else anyway. For deep-frying, find a good, deep pan with its own basket; a great many chip-pans seem very shallow, with a risk of the fat boiling over and causing a fire. Have at least one really heavy small frying-pan for omelettes, which can double as a pancake pan if necessary.

Of all the makes of vitrified ironware pans, Le Creuset still seem to me to be the best. Their range is very wide, from sauté pans with lids to a good series of oblong terrines, round and oval casseroles in many different sizes, and, particularly useful, gratin dishes which can double as frying pans. The quality is good, and their prices competitive. I have had many of my Le Creuset pans for a dozen years; their only sign of age being a comfortable brownish look to the white linings. As far as pottery casseroles go, for durability choose ovenproof porcelain (such as Royal Worcester) or stoneware (like that made by Pearson's of Chesterfield), rather than earthenware. Both stoneware and porcelain are fired at very high temperatures during their manufacture, giving them an extremely durable glaze which will not crack like an earthenware glaze. Stoneware has the same rustic charms, and is as cheap as earthenware; porcelain is more elegant, and more expensive, but conducts heat more efficiently. I use stoneware for long slow cooking, and porcelain for *gratins*, and for baking fish.

I recommend carbon steel knives. Even the best stainless steel knife cannot be honed to the razor sharpness of a carbon steel blade, and this quality more than repays the extra care required to stop carbon steel from rusting. Thorough drying should be enough for knives you use frequently; a few drops of cooking oil on a paper towel rubbed over the blades of knives you use less frequently will keep them in good condition. Although there are many good makes of carbon steel knives on the market, some of my own favourites have been bought for a few pence from junk shops: a ham knife with a long flexible blade, a perfectly balanced carving knife with a deeply grooved horn handle to prevent slipping and numerous small knives, particularly useful for boning meat. Keep sharp knives in a rack, rather than in a drawer, where they quickly become blunt as they jostle against other implements – they are also more easy to get at. Use stainless steel knives for preparing fruit, or any vegetable, such as avocado pears, which discolours easily, and keep one with a serrated blade for slicing tomatoes.

Chopping boards and blocks should be of thick wood without joins – have at least two. A pastry board isn't really necessary if you have a wooden kitchen table, but if all your work surfaces are of laminated plastic, then you will need one, as pastry seems to stick to a plastic surface. Marble is the best of all surfaces for rolling pastry. Junk shops sometimes sell pieces of marble from old washstands fairly cheaply.

Baking equipment should include one or two really heavy baking sheets which will remain flat when put into a hot oven; a wire cooling rack; two sizes of hinged cake tin with removable bases; a pair of non-stick sponge tins; a non-stick bun tin; a pair of flan tins, also with removable bases. If you are going to make bread, non-stick bread tins are a great help, but not essential.

For weighing and measuring, the old-fashioned scales with a shallow pan and separate weights are still the most reliable method; have two sets of weights now, one metric. A set of plastic spoons, or, preferably, aluminium ones if you can get them, is useful. Have one or two measuring jugs for liquids.

A forest of wooden spoons, in a jar by the cooker, is vital; include a wooden fork for stirring *risotto* without breaking up the softened rice, and for hooking pasta out of the pan to see if it is cooked. A wooden spatula for scraping bowls and saucepans is also handy. I keep a balloon whisk in the same jar, for rescuing lumpy sauces.

My ideal electric mixer has yet to be invented. The most recent model has almost all the necessary virtues; it is compact, reasonably quiet, sieves, blends, chops, purées, and is aesthetically pleasing, but it doesn't whisk egg-whites – a serious omission in a family which enjoys soufflés and meringues. Provided you have enough space, the Kenwood Chef is still perhaps the best buy. You can add the various accessories as you find you need them, such as the dough hook if you make a lot of bread, or the sausage-making attachment for the mincer, or the potato peeler if your family is large. The liquidizer is particularly efficient. I do prefer to use a vegetable-mill (*mouli-légumes*) for soups, however, and for making fruit purées. Its near relation, the *mouli-juliénne*, is invaluable for slicing and shredding vegetables for all sorts of dishes.

Strainers and drainers are very important. Keep as many sieves and colanders in the kitchen as you have room for. I use old pillow-cases for straining jellies and stocks. They are just as efficient as old fashioned jelly-bags and do not take up as much space as large nylon sieves. They can also be thoroughly washed in the washing-machine, then folded away in a drawer. If you find a flat china drainer (sometimes decorated with transfer designs) in a junk shop, buy it and see how useful it is for draining artichokes and asparagus, or meat before it is potted (*see* the recipe for *rillettes* on page 59). A salad basket is invaluable for drying off lettuce, and there is a particularly good one, based on the spinning-top principle, which spins out the water without bruising the leaves.

Small gadgets – garlic crushers, lemon zesters, olive-stoners, larding-needles – may not be used often, but are always handy. I like to have at least four pepper-grinders; one for the table, one for the kitchen, one for coriander and one for allspice. Choose a really good-quality professional grinder for the kitchen, as that one will probably do the most work, and there is nothing more irritating than a half-hearted pepper mill. A *demi-lune* or *mezze-luna* (a semi-circular blade with one or two handles and its own wooden chopping dish) is useful for all sorts of small chopping jobs when it is not worth using a blender or mincer – it is easy to clean, too. If your cooker is surrounded by laminated plastic surfaces, have one or two wooden saucepan stands nearby on which to rest pans straight off the stove.

Kitchen haberdashery deserves a drawer to itself – string, linen thread and a darning-needle for sewing up poultry, wooden skewers (butchers will sometimes sell you these), foil, cling-wrap, waxed or greaseproof paper, Bakewell paper for lining cake tins and cooking meringues, and muslin, which has a million uses. It can still be bought from old-fashioned drapers (Limericks, of Westcliff-on-Sea, Essex, sell it by post, as well as other useful kitchen drapery, including really thick and efficient oven-cloths, and large aprons), or you can buy Indian cheesecloth. Alternatively, old muslin nappies, or men's handkerchiefs, well-boiled, will do just as well. Keep plenty of polythene bags, especially if you have a freezer, and save margarine tubs and yoghurt pots for keeping leftovers in the fridge.

Finally, my favourite piece of kitchen equipment is a fish-smoker. I would never have thought of buying it for myself, but it is a present which I would choose again and again. It is very compact and runs on methylated spirits and smoke-dust (to be bought from wherever you bought the smoker itself – Habitat stock them; so do sports shops specializing in fishing tackle). You can add all sorts of dried herbs to the smoke-dust to vary the flavour, and sausages, cod's roe (for taramasalata), pieces of duck, chicken or pork all respond as well as fish to being smoked in it. I would add that it is a cosmetic, rather than a preservative process. Anything smoked in this way should be eaten fairly quickly, or stored in the freezer.

Grow-it-Yourself

Grow - it -Yourself

If you do have enough space to grow one or two vegetables, then choose those that are almost impossible to buy fresh and cheap.

FRUIT

Soft fruit travels badly, and even though new strains are being developed (*e.g.* more durable raspberries), it is almost always at the expense of flavour. A few raspberry canes (a variety like 'Malling Promise' is a good one) do not take up much room, and will repay you handsomely.

Strawberries, on the other hand, do need space, and are back-breaking to pick. It is easier to organize a family picking at a strawberry farm in July, and then to turn them into jam, ice-cream and sorbets to last through the winter. Alpine strawberries, however, have a wonderful flavour, are no trouble to grow, and can be used as very pretty ground-cover too. 'Baron Solemacher' is a variety which can be used as an edging plant, as it does not produce runners, remaining a compact, decorative and productive plant for many years.

Black, white and redcurrants all need space, but one bush of each will produce three-currant tart, blackcurrant ice-cream, white-currant jelly and redcurrant jam. You can make a magical sorbet out of the leaves before the fruit even appears (*see* page 153).

SUMMER VEGETABLES

It is worth devoting a small area to *mange-tout* or sugar peas. They are wonderfully labour-saving, as you eat pods and all. When large and tough they make good soup.

Broad beans are worth growing yourself, too; then you can pick them small enough to cook whole, in their pods, like French beans.

The bean-tops (picked out when the plants are flowering to discourage black-fly and encourage the crop), are very good cooked like spinach (*see* page 142). 'The Midget' is a good dwarf variety, with plenty of flavour, for small gardens. Runner beans are decorative enough to be grown round a kitchen window, provided they get enough sun, and enough moisture in dry weather. You can then avoid the monster beans at the greengrocer's. Suttons sell a variety called 'Sunset', which has pale pink flowers; they claim 'outstanding flavour'.

There is not always much point in growing your own lettuces unless you are a long way from any supply, but they are always better fresh out of the ground. They, too, can be grown as edging plants, and 'Buttercrunch' is a crisp variety with good flavour, which doesn't run to seed so quickly.

Tomatoes are an obvious choice for anyone with a sunny patch. Choose an outdoor bush variety with plenty of flavour, and grow them from seed if you can, as plants offered for sale are, more often than not, of the high-cropping, flavourless varieties like 'Money-maker' or 'Eurocross'. Suttons' 'French Cross' is very good. If you do choose to buy plants and grow them in one of the many types of compost-bags, don't expect a cheap crop; pound for pound, they will cost the same as, or more than those bought from the green-grocer.

If you live far from a good supply of garlic, it might be worthwhile growing your own. The further north you are, the warmer and more sheltered the growing area will have to be in order to produce fat and pungent bulbs. Suttons and Dobies sell garlic for planting, or you can split your cooking garlic into cloves and plant those. Plant them pointed end up about ½" deep and 6" apart. Harvest the garlic when the leaves turn yellow.

Globe artichokes are my favourite of all summer vegetables. The fine plants can look beautiful in a sunny herbaceous border, and as perennials they will need little attention beyond the provision of some manure if you can get it, and splitting them when the plants get too big. Scotts of Merriott in Somerset stock globe artichokes; so do A. R. Paske Ltd., Regal Lodge, Kentford, Newmarket, Suffolk. The most popular variety is 'Gros Vert de Laon', which produces spherical green heads, but I prefer the flavour of 'Grand Camus de Bretagne', which is purplish and more conical in shape. If you can bear to leave one or two heads on the plants, allow them to flower; then pick and dry them for the winter. In a hot summer, they will smell so strongly of honey that two in a vase will scent a whole room.

It is undoubtedly hard work growing potatoes, and they do need space, and generous watering in dry summers. In spite of these problems, however, there are several continental varieties worth growing for flavour and texture. Pink Fir Apple is a delicious red oblong potato with nutty yellow flesh; it makes very good salads, and is also useful for a true *gratin dauphinois*. Seed potatoes are stocked by Phoenix Distributors Ltd., 15 Great George Street, Bristol, and also by Captain D. Maclean, Dornock Farm, Crieff, Perthshire. He also stocks Bintje, another good salad potato, and Aura, which is similar to Pink Fir Apple in texture and flavour. Captain Maclean's list makes fascinating reading for the gardener – it contains nearly 200 different varieties of potato – but it is frustrating for the cook, as no culinary qualities are mentioned at all; Kipfler, another delicious 'salad type' is simply labelled WLM, or White, Long, Main-crop. This list is available from October onwards – send a stamped addressed envelope. The continental varieties are more expensive than the more mundane ones, so it is worth keeping some of your crop back to use as seed the following year. You will be able to do this successfully for only two or three years, but it does help to defray the cost. I find that growing a small amount of one of these continental varieties is well worth the trouble, but I doubt if it is worth digging up the lawn to grow King Edwards.

HERBS

Much has been written about growing herbs and I don't think that anyone who cooks can doubt that the use of fresh herbs promotes food into the realms of *cuisine soignée*. Equally, home-dried herbs are much better than bought ones, and very much more satisfying to use. Even in a town garden there is no problem; bay trees grow well in tubs, thyme can be grown between paving stones, rosemary and sage positively appreciate poor soil (though they do need sun). Fennel, particularly bronze fennel, lovage and chives look well in flower beds.

Chervil seems to survive all but the most severe winters. It is, strictly speaking, an annual, but seeds itself with such fervour that one packet of seeds should last you a lifetime. Its fresh aniseed flavour is very welcome in the winter, especially as it is too delicate to withstand drying. French tarragon *(artemisia dracunculus)* should be grown in a large pot so that it can be brought in in winter. Russian tarragon is much hardier but has little flavour. Sweet basil *(ocimum basilicum)* is a sun-loving annual best grown in small pots on a south-facing window-sill or in a greenhouse. In late summer and early autumn the stalks will begin to go brown at the base. Harvest the top branches rapidly and put two or three pieces into a bottle of red wine vinegar to make basil vinegar for the winter – very good in stews and jugged hare. Chop the rest finely, mix it with grated Parmesan and freeze in small quantities to season pasta dishes, or to use as the basis for *pesto* (a sauce made from basil, cheese, olive oil and pine nuts). It loses much of its flavour when dried.

Thyme, marjoram, sage, rosemary and bayleaves all dry well between sheets of newspaper in an airing-cupboard. Once dried, they should be stored away from light and air. Small calico bags with draw-strings, like miniature shoe-bags, with the name of the herb written on the front with a laundry marker, make an ideal method for storing herbs. They can be hung on a hook near the cooker, and washed before re-using the next season.

WINTER VEGETABLES

My ideal winter vegetable garden consists of rows of leeks, parsley, and 'Sugarloaf' chicory, planted alternately. The contrasting shapes of these three plants, and their fresh greenness in the drab winter months, is a far more pleasing sight from the kitchen window than ranks of knobbly brassicas, quite apart from their culinary values. Leeks have so many uses, as flavouring, as well as being delicious vegetables in their own right, that they are worth growing yourself; it is an advantage to be able to dig them up while they are young and slim, to cook *à la grecque* and also not to have to pay for the tough dark green leaves always left on by the greengrocer. Parsley is invaluable in the winter; its refreshingly sharp iron flavour brightens up potato purées and vegetable soups. Now that the white heads of forced chicory cost something approaching £1 a pound, it is useful to know that 'Sugarloaf' has the same bitter taste, and the same crisp texture, but can be grown very easily, without blanching, and seems to be able to withstand several days of very hard frost, even in the north, without severe damage to the hearts. Seeds are available by post from Suttons Seeds Ltd, Hele Road, Torquay, Devon, and from Samuel Dobie & Son Ltd, Upper Dee Mills, Llangollen, Clwyd, although they sell it under the name 'Winter Fare'.

I never grow vegetables for the freezer, although I do, of course, freeze any surplus. The whole charm of vegetables is their seasonal variation and their compatibility with certain dishes: Brussels sprouts are delicious with game, but overpowering with spring lamb. Peas go well with veal chops but not with steak-and-kidney pudding. The deep-freeze revolution has brought a blurring of these seasonal pleasures, and I would happily forgo the convenience of frozen runner beans for the enjoyment of eating fresh ones.

Brew-it-
Yourself

Brew-it-Yourself

I am not an advocate of hedgerow wines; despite their interesting flavours they are often too sweet and leave one with a dire hangover that not even a good Burgundy would have made worthwhile. However, to have plenty of cooking wine on hand, you may wish to make wine from wine-kits using grape juice. Boots have tins of grape-juice with very clear, step-by-step instructions.

The only hedgerow wine for which I make an exception is elderflower. It used to be known as English 'Frontignan', and certainly it does have a remarkably good muscatel flavour. An elder-bush can be a most useful item in any garden, as both the flowers and fruit produce delicious and unusual drinks and sweet dishes. I have a friend who often adds elderberries to her fruit salads, where their sharp, refreshing flavour and dark colouring punctuate the more ordinary ingredients most agreeably. Elderflower wine, not too sweet and well-chilled, can be a good dessert wine, is very good as a basis for fruit syrups, and makes one of the best of all sorbets (*see* recipe for blackcurrant leaf sorbet, page 153).

Miss Hess's Elderflower Wine

To each gallon of water add 6 large elderflower heads, fully out, Stir in 1½ lb caster sugar, the rind and juice of a lemon and 2 tblsps of white wine vinegar. Bring all to the boil, withdraw from the heat and leave to stand for 36 hours. Strain through muslin, then bottle in strong bottles with corks, not screw-tops. Keep for a month before drinking.

Alternatively, infuse 4 elderflower heads in 6 pints of hot water, until you have a good flavour from the flowers. Cool to lukewarm and use this infusion to make up a tin of white grape juice, following the directions of the label for making ordinary white wine.

The summer of 1977 was wonderful for raspberries, and a large home-grown crop prompted me to try the following two Edwardian recipes.

Raspberry Brandy

8 oz freshly picked raspberries
¾ pint cheap grape brandy
2 in bruised cinnamon stick

Rind of ½ a lemon in strips
Rind of ½ an orange in strips
4 oz caster sugar

Mash the raspberries with a fork, stir in the orange and lemon rind, and the cinnamon. Pour over the brandy. Cover tightly and leave in a cool place for 48 hours. Strain through a muslin-lined sieve, then stir in the sugar until it dissolves. Bottle and cork well, and keep for at least three weeks before drinking. The discarded raspberry pulp makes a delicious ice-cream; remove the peel and cinnamon, stir in sugar to taste, then follow the recipe for damson ice-cream on page 153.

Raspberry Vinegar

1 lb raspberries
1 pint cider vinegar

12 oz caster sugar for each pint – about 15 oz are needed for this recipe

Crush the raspberries and add to the vinegar. Leave covered, in a cool place for a fortnight, stirring occasionally. Strain through muslin into a saucepan and add the sugar. Boil for 10 minutes, until the sugar has dissolved, then allow to get quite cold before bottling. To drink, put a teaspoonful in a glass of ice-cold water – it makes a wonderfully refreshing drink on a hot day. It is also comforting for colds when made with hot water. Elderberry or blackberry vinegars can be made in the same way.

Home-made wine vinegar is a marvellous by-product of wine dregs, but it can be difficult to start, as a 'culture' or 'mother' is needed, rather as with making yoghourt. You may be able to scrounge a *mère* from French friends, or you can try growing your own – a somewhat hit-or-miss affair, but well worth doing. The best way seems to be to leave the dregs of a good wine in their original bottle, in a warm, slightly humid place. Leave the bottle uncovered so that bacteria can form. Forget about it for at least a month, then tip the dregs very carefully into a basin. If a blob of jelly-like substance has formed, you have succeeded – that is the precious vinegar culture. Now all you have to do is to put this culture into a suitable container and feed it with wine dregs whenever you have them. Elizabeth David Ltd, of Bourne Street, London SW1, sells vinegar barrels which enable you to pour in dregs through a corked hole in the top of the barrel, and draw off the vinegar by a tap in the bottom; any tall glass jar will do – I use an old-fashioned Kilner jar with a narrow neck and glass lid. The vinegar produced by this method is so much nicer than any bought variety that it is very much a case of 'If at first you don't succeed ...' Keep the vinegar jar in as constant a temperature as possible of about 55-60° F.

Recipes

All recipes are for four healthy appetites, unless otherwise stated, and ingredients are generally listed in sequence.

Soups

Soups

It is not essential to have good stock for soup; initial slow cooking of the vegetables in butter helps, and so does the sparing use of a stock cube or powder, but good stock does contribute enormously to the quality of the final product.

When you do have good ingredients for stock, such as meat, poultry or game bones, leek tops, carrots, onions, parsley stalks and outside sticks of celery, make the most of them. If you have a freezer, large quantities can be boiled down until very concentrated, then frozen in ice-cube trays, removed and stored in labelled poly-thene bags. One stock cube will make a pint of fresh stock. Fish stock can be made from trimmings bought very cheaply from the fish monger (he might even give them away) then concentrated and frozen in the same way.

When making stock from poultry carcases, game or meat bones, do not be tempted to let them boil for too long in the hope of getting more flavour out of them. The only flavour you will end up with is that of boiled bone. Cover the bones and flavouring vegetables with cold water, add a little salt and bring *slowly* to the boil. This will help draw the flavour out of the ingredients into the liquid. Once boiling, lower the heat and leave the pan to simmer for about half-an-hour. Leaving the skins on onions used for flavouring will give the stock a good golden colour.

Be ruthless about throwing away very salt stock left from cooking ham or a salt duck; nothing will stop it from making very salty soup.

Reboil stock every other day in summer, if you cannot store it in the freezer, and strain out any vegetables as these will make it go bad more quickly.

Basic Winter Vegetable Soup

2 carrots	2 oz butter
2 sliced onions	1 teasp salt
2 sticks celery	2 pints stock
1 parsnip	1 bayleaf
½ swede	½ pint milk
2 leeks	

Peel and slice all the vegetables. Melt the butter in a heavy pan, add the vegetables and a teaspoon of salt, stir well, cover the pan and leave, over a gentle heat, until the vegetables are soft. Add the hot stock and the bayleaf, bring rapidly to the boil and simmer until the vegetables are well cooked. Remove the bayleaf and put the soup through the vegetable-mill. Heat the milk, and, just before it boils, stir it into the soup. Taste for seasoning, and add pepper, and salt if needed. You can finish the soup by adding finely chopped parsley and celery leaves, or cubes of crisply fried bacon, and chopped garlic, or simply with a knob of butter.

Old-Fashioned Mushroom Soup

1 lb mushrooms	in milk (use good bread,
1 small onion	not sliced-and-wrapped)
2 oz butter	2 pints stock
2 thick slices white bread,	2 tblsps dry sherry
without the crusts, soaked	A little thick cream

Chop the onion finely and melt it in the butter over a low heat. Chop the mushrooms, add them to the onion and cook gently until the juices run. Squeeze the milk from the bread and beat it into the mushrooms until they are well mixed. Pour in the stock, stirring as you do so, add a pinch of salt, cover the pan and simmer for 20 minutes. Cool, then liquidize. Add the sherry and taste for seasoning. Stir in the cream, and serve with a little chopped parsley.

Vegetable Chowder

8 oz salt belly pork
  (*see* page 10)
1 oz butter
2 cloves garlic
3 medium-sized potatoes
3 leeks

6 sticks celery
About ¼ pint stock
1 pint milk
2 bayleaves
A little chopped watercress
  and parsley

Cut the pork into cubes and frizzle them in the butter in a heavy pan. Bruise the garlic and add it to the pork. Peel the potatoes and cut into rough cubes, slice the leeks and celery finely. Add to the pan, stir well and cook gently for 10 minutes. Pour on the hot stock (it should only just cover the pork and vegetables – add a little water if necessary) and simmer for about ½ hour, or until the potatoes and leeks are soft but the celery still has a bite to it. Bring the milk and bayleaves to the boil in a separate pan and pour into the chowder. Mix well and taste – season fairly highly with lots of freshly ground pepper, a little grated nutmeg, and salt, taking the saltiness of the pork into account. Sprinkle with freshly chopped watercress and parsley and serve in large bowls with plenty of fresh bread and butter. Very good for a winter lunch.

Cream of Leek and Cauliflower Soup

3 leeks – white part only
1 small cauliflower
1 oz butter

½ pint light stock
1 pint hot milk
Salt, pepper, nutmeg

Soften the finely sliced leeks in the butter, then add the cauliflower (broken into flowerets). Mix thoroughly and cook gently for 10 minutes. Add the hot stock and simmer for 20 minutes, or until the vegetables are soft. Put in the liquidizer and blend until smooth, then return the soup to the pan and add the hot milk. Season with salt, pepper and a little grated nutmeg, then reheat without boiling. Add a spoonful of thick cream to each bowlful. This is a rich, bland winter soup, good before a strong dish such as game.

Game Soup

The head and ribs of a hare – keep the rest for jugging	*Bouquet garni* of thyme, orange rind and parsley stalks
1 pigeon, plucked and drawn	Salt
Good dripping	4 whole peppercorns
2 carrots	2 tblsps flour
2 large onions, stuck with 4 cloves	1 wineglass port
	Redcurrant jelly
3 pints stock or water	*Croûtons*

Heat about 2 oz beef, duck or pork dripping in a large saucepan. Brown the hare pieces and the pigeon all over. Add the carrots, split but unpeeled, the onions, the *bouquet garni* and the cold stock or water. Stir in a little salt and the peppercorns, and bring slowly to the boil, stirring often to mix in the residue left on the bottom of the pan after browning the meat. Simmer briskly, with the lid half off, for about ¾ of an hour, or until the stock has a good flavour.

Melt 1 tablespoon of dripping in another pan, and stir in the flour. Cook until the flour is brown, taking care not to let it burn. Add the strained stock, a little at a time as if making a white sauce and, stirring constantly, bring the soup to the boil and simmer for about 15 minutes. Add the port and redcurrant jelly to taste (do not make it too sweet) and serve very hot with *croûtons* fried in the same dripping you used for the soup. For a more filling soup, add the meat picked from the hare and pigeon and cut into small pieces.

Good stock, good dripping and long cooking are all necessary for the best onion soups. Slow simmering brings out the sweet mellow flavour of the onions best. As I think 'French' onion soup, with its stringy cheese and soggy bread is somewhat overrated, here is a patriotic English recipe:

English Onion Soup

2 oz good beef dripping	3 cloves
1 lb mild English onions	2 pints beef stock
1 teasp sugar	Salt and pepper

Melt the dripping and fry one of the onions, finely sliced, to a dark golden brown. DO NOT LET IT BURN. Add the sugar and let it caramelize with the onion, watching carefully. Lower the heat, and add the rest of the onions, also finely sliced, and the cloves. Stir well, cover the pan and let them cook slowly for about 20 minutes. Add the stock and a little salt and simmer very gently for 1 hour (you can do this in a low oven, if you have it on already). Taste, check for seasoning, adding plenty of freshly-ground pepper and more salt, if necessary. Remove the cloves, if you can find them, and serve very, very hot. The soup should be a lovely dark golden brown from the caramelizing process, and slightly spicy.

Cream of Onion Soup

1 lb mild onions   ½ pint milk
2 small potatoes   Salt, pepper,
2 oz butter   a blade of mace
2 pints light stock

Soften the peeled and sliced onions and potatoes in the butter, over a low heat, for about 20 minutes. Add the stock and the blade of mace and simmer for ¾ of an hour. Cool the soup a little, then pour it into the blender and blend until smooth. Meanwhile, heat the milk in the soup pan and pour the liquidized soup slowly into the milk, whisking lightly with a fork or balloon whisk as you do so. Season with salt, a little pepper, and a little extra powdered mace if you think it needs it.

Caraway Soup

This is a curious but delicious middle-European soup with definite charm for caraway-seed lovers. It is an excellent soup for post-Christmas indigestion and like onion soup depends on good stock for its success.

2 tblsps caraway seeds   1½ pints beef or game stock
1 oz butter   Salt
½ oz flour   A little freshly ground pepper

Melt the butter in a pan and add the caraway seeds; leave them to sizzle over a medium heat for 5 minutes. Remove from the heat and stir in the flour. Return to the heat and cook the flour until brown; add the hot stock very slowly, stirring briskly. Simmer for 15 minutes, strain out the caraway seeds through a sieve, and season to taste with salt and pepper. Serve very hot, with a spoonful of cold sour cream in the middle of each bowl.

Celery Soup with Chervil

1 small onion
2 small potatoes
5 large sticks celery
A few parsley stalks

2 oz butter
2 pints stock
1 tblsp chopped fresh chervil

Peel and chop the onion and potatoes, and slice the celery. Melt the butter and add the vegetables, together with a little salt, and the parsley stalks. Cook gently until the vegetables have absorbed the butter. Pour on the hot stock and simmer until all the vegetables are cooked. Put it through the fine disk on the vegetable-mill. At this stage you can add ½ pint of hot milk, if you want a creamier soup, but be sure to scald it first, as celery has a tendency to curdle milk if it is added cold. Adjust the seasoning and serve with plenty of finely chopped chervil; 2 tablespoons of thick cream will improve it further.

Richard Bradley's Green Pease Soup

'Boil a Quart of old Pease tender in a Quart of Water, bruise them, and strain the pulp through a Sieve, and in the same Water boil a Quart of young Pease, and when enough add to them the Pulp of the old ones, a little Spinage, Mint, Sorrel, Lettuce, and a half a Pound of melted Butter, with a little of the Liquor; shake a little Flour into it, let it boil; and mingle all well together, to serve it with toasted Bread' From *The Country Housewife*, 1753.

Richard Bradley's recipe is delicious; use dried peas, soaked, then cooked until tender and put through the *mouli*. You can use frozen peas for his 'young Pease', but try to use all the other vegetables. I use half that amount of butter, and no flour, as the dried peas are floury enough.

Seaside Bouillabaisse

One of the delights of holiday shrimping expeditions is the harvest of all sorts of small fish and crustaceans scooped up in the net along with the shrimps themselves. When sorting out the largest shrimps for boiling, transfer all the miscellaneous fish and the tiny shrimps to another saucepan. Discard any of the large yellow crabs – they are supposed to be poisonous – and cover the rest with water. Add a little salt, bring to a rolling boil and skim off the scum that rises. Simmer for about 45 minutes, then push the panful of fish through the *mouli*. You will now have an unseasoned but excellent fish broth.

1 large onion	Salt and pepper
4 cloves garlic	2 egg yolks
Olive oil	Wine vinegar
1 large tin tomatoes	Crushed garlic
About 2½ pints fish broth	Paprika
Bouquet garni of thyme, fennel and parsley stalks	

Soften the sliced onion and garlic in about 2 tblsps olive oil, then add the tomatoes and the fish broth. Bring to the boil, throw in the *bouquet*, season with a little salt and pepper and simmer for 20 minutes.

Make a thick mayonnaise from the egg yolks, beaten with a few drops of vinegar and a little salt. Add about ¼ pint olive oil, drop by drop until the mixture thickens, then in a thin stream until you have the right consistency, beating hard all the time. Season with paprika and crushed garlic. Put a spoonful of this mayonnaise into each bowl before pouring in large ladlesful of soup. Garnish with a few cooked and peeled shrimps.

A similar, but paler, version can be made from fish-trimmings from your fishmonger. It will be good, but will lack the wonderful flavour of the fresh-from-the-sea mixture of flounders, dabs. crabs, shrimps and other small fry.

Smoked Haddock Soup

This soup cheats somewhat as it simply uses up the milk in which you have cooked smoked haddock for another dish – like kedgeree.

1 lb smoked haddock (Finnan is best)	1½ pints milk
2 bayleaves	Pepper

Cover the haddock with the milk, add the bayleaves and one turn of the peppermill. Simmer very gently until the fish is cooked, then remove it and set aside for another dish. Strain the milk, and taste to see how salty it is.

1 small carrot	1 oz butter
1 small onion	4 chopped parsley

Chop the onion and carrot and melt them in the butter over a low heat until soft. Add the haddock milk slowly, and a very little salt if it needs it. Simmer gently until the vegetables are cooked. Put it through the *mouli* and taste for seasoning again. Sprinkle with chopped parsley.

Gazpacho with Hot Sausages

This makes a good summer lunch. The sausages should be small and highly seasoned; Marks & Spencer's herb pork chipolatas twisted into half their size will do.

1 lb tomatoes	3 oz white breadcrumbs
1 small cucumber	3 tblsps olive oil
1 small onion	Salt and freshly ground pepper
2 cloves garlic	1 lb sausages
1 green pepper	Chopped fresh basil

Peel the tomatoes by pouring boiling water over them, and leaving them until the skins split. Cut them into rough pieces. Peel and chop the cucumber, and the onion and garlic. Cut the pepper in half, remove the seeds and white pith. Put all the ingredients, except for the oil, basil, and of course, the sausages, into the blender and blend for a little – do not make too smooth a mixture. With the blender at a slow speed, gradually add the oil. Season with plenty of salt and pepper. Chill the gazpacho in the fridge for at least 2 hours, wrapping the bowl entirely in foil to keep the smell of garlic from tainting everything else in the fridge. The soup should be a thick purée, but if you feel it is too thick, thin it with a little iced water. Do not add the basil until you are ready to eat.

About 20 minutes before serving, fry the sausages – gently at first so that they do not burst, raising the heat at the end to brown them well. Drain them and transfer them to a heated serving dish. Add the basil to the gazpacho. If possible, keep the sausages hot at table on a table-heater or in a fondue pan. Give each person a bowl of icy gazpacho, and a fork with which to spear the sausages; so that they can take alternate mouthfuls of the cold soup and piping hot sausage.

Tomato and Orange Soup

1½ lb fresh tomatoes   1 teasp whole coriander
2 large juicy oranges   1½ pints chicken stock
1 small onion   Salt and pepper

Cut up the tomatoes without bothering to remove the skins or pips. Slice one of the oranges into thick slices. Chop the onion. Crush the coriander lightly. Put all these ingredients, the stock and a little salt and pepper into a pan and bring slowly to the boil. Simmer until the onion is soft, then put through the vegetable-mill. Chill and serve with a spoonful of whipped cream on top of each bowlful, and an orange wedge to squeeze in the soup as you drink it.

Pea-pod Soup

This is a good way to make use of the juicy pea-pods it always seems such a waste to throw away. A vegetable-mill is essential, or you will have to sieve your soup after liquidizing it.

The pods from 2 lb fresh peas   Pinch sugar
1 small onion   Salt and pepper
3 oz butter   Cream and chopped chervil
2 pints stock

Melt the onion in the butter, then pour on the stock. Throw in the washed pods, bring to the boil, add the salt and sugar and simmer until the pods are soft. Put through the *mouli*. Reheat and taste for seasoning; stir in the cream and fresh chervil and serve at once. You can add a few cooked peas at the end as well if you have them.

Runner Bean Soup with Ham

1 lb medium-sized runner beans	2 pints stock – ham, if it is not too salty
2 onions	2 oz rice
3 cloves garlic	¼ pint single cream
2 oz butter	¾ lb piece of cooked ham

Remove any strings from the runner beans with a potato peeler or sharp knife, then slice them into thick pieces. Do not shred them. Melt the butter in a heavy pan, add the finely chopped onions and garlic, and the beans. Let them all absorb the butter over a gentle heat for about 10 minutes, with a lid on the pan. Add the stock, and bring to the boil, then simmer for about 10 minutes. Throw in the washed rice and simmer until the rice is cooked. The beans should be cooked at about the same time, but they can be left a little underdone with advantage. Bring the cream to the boil in a separate pan and add to the soup. Cut the ham into cubes and add these too. Reheat the soup without boiling – check for seasoning after the addition of the cream and ham. Sprinkle with any chopped fresh herbs. A beautiful pink, green and white soup, substantial enough for lunch.

Chicken Broth with Liver Dumplings

1 3 lb boiling fowl	thyme, bayleaf, rosemary and a strip of lemon peel
4 oz shin beef	
4 large carrots, split	3 large onions
A large sprig of herbs – celery leaves, parsley stalks,	3 leeks
	6 crushed peppercorns

DUMPLINGS

2 oz fresh breadcrumbs	1 finely chopped chicken liver
2 oz suet	2 tblsps finely chopped fresh
2 oz plain flour	herbs
Pinch baking powder	1 small beaten egg
Salt and pepper	

Watercress

Put all the soup ingredients (making sure the leeks are free from grit) into a large pan including the *whole* chicken, and cover with cold water. Add 2 teaspoons salt and bring very slowly to the boil. Lower the heat and cook gently until the chicken is tender (you can also do this in a low oven – 250° F). The time this takes very much depends on the age of the chicken; if it is a really old boiling fowl it will need at least 2½ hours.

Meanwhile, make the dumplings: mix all the ingredients in a bowl, bind with the beaten egg and form into small balls, about the size of a walnut. Cover and keep until needed.

When the chicken is cooked, remove it and the beef to a warm plate, cover with foil and put in a low oven to keep hot. Strain the broth and taste it, seasoning accordingly. Bring it to the boil, add the dumplings, cover the pan and simmer fast for ½ hour. Serve the broth and dumplings with chopped watercress. The chicken and beef, with a *salsa verde* (*see* page 64) and baked potatoes, will make a very good second course.

First Courses ~
Light Lunches &
Supper Dishes!

First Courses, Light Lunches and Supper Dishes

As many *hors d'oeuvres* dishes can be magnified and used for lunches and suppers, I have included them all in one chapter.

EGGS

Eggs are the most versatile and convenient food imaginable and with a dozen in the larder you need never be at a loss; despite their increase in price over the last few years, they still seem to be remarkably good value. A fresh boiled egg, with good brown bread and plenty of butter, makes one of the simplest lunches of all.

Oeufs mollets are simply boiled eggs dressed up – or, rather, undressed – as you remove the shells before serving them in any one of a number of ways. You will need one egg per person for a first course, two each for a main dish. In order to time a number of eggs exactly, which is important, put them all into a saucepan and pour boiling water over them. Cook for exactly 5 minutes from the time you add the water, then add a cupful of cold water to stop them cooking all together. Drain them and let them get cool enough to handle. Prepare the sauce while they are cooling. Tap each egg all over a hard surface, to crack and loose the shell, then peel carefully. Put the shelled eggs into the waiting sauce (which should be in a fire-proof *gratin* dish which you can take straight to table), and turn them over in it until they are reheated, but no further cooked.

Oeufs Mollets with Herbs and Butter

A very simple dish for which fresh herbs are a necessity. Chop finely a combination of 2 or 3 or more of the following herbs: chervil, parsley, tarragon, chives, fennel and basil. Melt a large lump of butter (about 1 oz for each egg) in a *gratin* dish over a low heat, stir in the herbs, and a little salt if the butter is unsalted. Put in the eggs and turn them over once or twice in the herb butter. Add a little freshly-ground pepper and serve with brown bread.

Eggs with Peas and Cream

For 4 eggs you will need ¼ pint thick cream, 1 large cupful of cooked peas, 1 teasp chopped chervil, salt and pepper. Put all the ingredients, except the eggs, into the *gratin* dish and simmer gently; add the eggs and heat gently, turning them over carefully once or twice.

Eggs with Garlic and Tomatoes

For 4 eggs peel and chop 3 tomatoes. Cook 2 chopped cloves of garlic in 1 oz butter until soft, add the tomatoes, salt and pepper and cook quickly until thick – too much cooking will spoil the fresh flavour. Put in the eggs, heat and serve with a sprinkling of basil or oregano, and garlic bread.

Eggs with Sorrel

Remove any tough stalks from a double handful of sorrel, and wash it thoroughly. Melt 2 oz butter in a small pan and put in the sorrel, drained, but with a little water left on the leaves. Put a lid on the pan and cook until the sorrel is tender. Season with salt and freshly-ground pepper and put into a *gratin* dish. Add a little thick cream, but heat it first, or it might curdle. Add the eggs to this sauce. If you cannot get sorrel, use spinach instead; then you will have a sort of *oeufs florentines*.

Eggs with Sauce Soubise

A mild and soothing supper dish. Cook 2 large chopped onions in 2 oz butter until soft. Add a tablespoon of flour, and ½ pint hot milk gradually, to make a thick onion sauce. Cook this sauce for a further ½ hour, then liquidize it in the blender, or put it through the vegetable-mill. Taste for seasoning, adding salt, freshly ground pepper and nutmeg. Pour about two-thirds of the sauce into the *gratin* dish, put in the shelled eggs, pour on the rest of the sauce and brown quickly under a very hot grill.

Omelettes have had so much written about them that there is really nothing more to add, but here is one unusual recipe which is very good for a filling lunch on a cold day.

Bread and Cheese Omelette

6 eggs	Butter and oil
3 slices bread, brown or white	Salt and pepper
2 oz Gruyère or Cheddar cheese	

Remove the crusts from the bread, cut it into cubes and fry until very crisp and brown in a mixture of butter and oil (the oil will stop the butter from burning at the high temperature needed to fry the bread crisp). Drain these *croûtons* on kitchen paper and set aside. Grate the cheese and mix with the *croûtons*. Make the omelettes in the usual way (eggs lightly beaten with salt and freshly ground pepper, poured into a really hot pan lightly greased with butter). When each one is just set underneath and still runny in the middle, add a tablespoonful or two of the bread and cheese mixture. Fold the omelette over and serve at once. The above quantity will make 4 omelettes.

Cold omelettes make delicious *hors d'oeuvres* and picnic food. The fillings should be simple – chopped fresh herbs, a slice of ham, or even a pat of unsalted butter. Do not make the omelettes too long before they are needed – about an hour, so that they can cool without getting leathery. A good picnic version of the American 'BLT' (bacon, lettuce and tomato sandwich) can be made as follows: for each person butter a large bap and line it with lettuce. Slip a cold omelette containing a crisply fried rasher of bacon and a few slices of tomato seasoned with salt, into each bap. You can add a spoonful of Hellman's mayonnaise for the real American touch.

Claudia Roden, in her lovely book *Middle Eastern Food* classes *eggah* as a sort of omelette, but, as she says, this is misleading. It is much more solid than the French version, and is perhaps more like a Spanish omelette, in which eggs are used like mortar to bind a number of ingredients. It can be cooked on top of the stove, in a *gratin* dish, or in the oven, which takes slightly longer. Like Mrs Roden, I prefer to cook it on top of the stove as it is easier to check on its consistency. *Eggah* should be quite firm, even in the middle, so that it can be cut into slices when cold.

Broad Bean and Lamb Eggah

4 eggs	1 teasp chopped marjoram
About 12 oz cold lamb,	Salt and pepper
chopped or minced	Butter
8 oz young shelled broad	
beans	

Beat the eggs lightly in a large bowl. Blanch the beans for 5 minutes in boiling water and drain well. Add the beans, lamb, marjoram, salt and pepper to the eggs in the bowl and mix thoroughly. Melt a lump of butter in a large *gratin* dish or frying pan, and, with a brush or wooden spoon, coat the sides of the pan with the butter as well. Pour in the *eggah* mixture. Cover the pan with a lid of foil and cook over a very low heat until the eggs have set – about 20-25 minutes. When the *eggah* is quite firm, remove it from the heat and put it under a very hot grill to brown the top. If you have been using a frying-pan, loosen the *eggah* and turn it out on to a warm plate before putting it under the grill. You can serve it cold, with a yoghourt and cucumber salad (*see* page 135), or cut it into wedges for picnic food. I like to serve it warm or hot, with more broad beans, cooked in butter and seasoned with black pepper and lemon juice.

The following is a rather more anglicized version, and uses the oven method of cooking. It is very good cold for a buffet lunch or supper.

Fish Eggah

4 oz prawns, in their shells	6 eggs
1 lb fresh mussels	1 tblsp chopped fennel
8 oz firm white fish	Salt, pepper, coriander

Shell the prawns and put the shells into a small pan; cover them
with ½ pint cold water, bring slowly to the boil, and simmer for
½ hour. Strain into a large pan. Scrub the mussels and remove their
beards. Put them into the pan with the prawn stock, cover it and
put it over a high heat. Cook fast, shaking the pan to distribute the
mussels, until all the shells are open. Line a colander with a piece
of muslin and tip the mussels into it, catching the stock as it drains
through, leaving behind any sand or mud. Poach the fish (cod, haddock or coley are all good) in this stock until it can be flaked with
the blade of a knife. Remove the mussels from their shells, and mix
them with the fish and add the prawns. Beat the eggs lightly and
stir them into the fish, together with the fennel, salt, pepper and
crushed coriander. Butter a shallow oven-proof dish and pour the
eggah mixture into it; cover it either with its own lid, or one made
of foil. Stand the dish in a baking-tin half full of water and bake at
350° F for about 45 minutes, or until the eggs are firm, even in the
centre. When cooked, allow the *eggah* to cool a little; loosen it with
a palette knife, put a plate over the top and invert the *eggah* on to
it. Brown it under a hot grill, then leave to cool. Surround it with
lemon wedges and serve it with a crisp salad. Use the fish stock for
soup, or freeze it in cubes.

La gougère is the Burgundian answer to the problem of how to drink
good wine with an egg *hors d'oeuvre*. It is really just a cheese *choux*
paste, and is extremely easy to make.

Les Gougères

2 oz butter	3 oz Gruyère, or mature
¼ pint water	Cheddar, cut into very
6 oz plain flour	small dice
3 egg yolks, or 2 whole eggs	Salt and pepper

Grease a heavy baking sheet, and heat the oven to 400° F. Put the butter and water into a saucepan and bring to the boil, in the meantime sifting the flour on to a sheet of greaseproof paper. When the butter and water have amalgamated and are boiling, draw the pan off the heat and shoot in the flour, all at once, beating hard. Beat until the paste leaves the sides and base of the pan clean. Beat in one egg, or egg yolk, at a time, until the paste is smooth and shiny. Add about two-thirds of the cheese, a little salt, and some freshly ground pepper, and beat again. Leave the mixture to cool. All this needs a strong arm, but you cannot go wrong as long as you beat the paste hard as you add the eggs.

Put a dessertspoonful of the paste on to the baking sheet and scatter a few cubes of cheese over each. Bake for 15-20 minutes, until puffy and golden, and serve very hot as a first course, with a good Burgundy.

La Gougère with Cheese Cream

Make the *gougère* paste as above, but form it into a circle on the baking sheet; sprinkle the cubes of cheese round the top. Bake at the same temperature, but for a little longer – about 25-30 minutes, or until a darker gold. Have ready the following mixture:

4 oz garlic and herb cream cheese (Boursin, or home-made *see* page 173).

¼ pint whipped cream   Salt and pepper, if necessary

Fold the cheese into the cream and season to taste. Give it plenty of time to chill in the fridge before using.

Slide the cooked *gougère* on to a plate and pile the cream cheese into the middle. Serve *immediately;* it is the contrast between the hot *gougère* and the very cold filling that is so good. White Burgundy goes well with this.

La Gougère with Leftover Meat or Game

This is one of the best ways of using up leftovers. First make the filling:

8 oz cooked meat, game or poultry	2 oz flour
1 small onion	½ pint stock
2 oz butter	2 tblsps mushroom ketchup
	Salt, pepper, nutmeg

Slice the onion thinly and melt it in the butter until soft. Stir in the flour, then add the warmed stock until you have a smooth sauce. Bring it to the boil, then simmer for about 15 minutes. Stir in the diced meat, mushroom ketchup, seasonings, and herbs appropriate to the type of meat you are using – tarragon for chicken, thyme for lamb, etc. Make the *gougère* paste as on page 51, butter a *gratin* dish and line the sides with two-thirds of the paste, using a wet spoon or knife to bank up the edges. Pour in the filling, and spoon the remaining third of paste over the top. Bake for 45 minutes at 375° F. A good supper dish.

Hard-boiled eggs are often mistreated. How often an egg mayonnaise appears as a grey-ringed, pallid and slippery egg shivering on a damp lettuce leaf, decorated with a blob of salad cream and the odd wisp of cress. Yet well-prepared egg mayonnaise can be very good indeed, and needs little effort, only a little care.

The first thing to remember is that it is over-cooking that causes the grey ring round the yolk. Put the eggs into a saucepan (prick each one with a pin at the pointed end if you want to avoid cracking), cover with cold water, add a pinch of salt, bring to the boil, then cook for exactly 10 minutes. Plunge the eggs immediately into cold water to stop them cooking further. Peel them when they are cool enough to handle. Eggs cooked like this have firm, not rubbery, whites, and set yolks which are nevertheless still creamy.

The mayonnaise should not be too solid – a light consistency combines best with the texture of hard-boiled eggs; to thin mayonnaise (*see* recipe on page 86), add a very little hot water, stirring all the time, until the right thickness is obtained. Season as you like; chopped tarragon is delicious with eggs in summer, as is chopped watercress in winter; quarter or halve the eggs and pour the mayonnaise over them, or put the mayonnaise in the middle and surround it with the eggs. Black olives make a good contrast both in colour and flavour.

VEGETABLES

One of the nicest ways of doing homage to home-grown produce is to serve it on its own, as a first course. I have named the following recipe after the house in which I first tasted it – served with home-made brown bread (and followed by huge helpings of roast lamb):

Leeks Ganthorpe

1 lb slim leeks	2-3 tblsps mayonnaise
French dressing	½ pint whipped cream
½ a small onion, finely chopped	

Remove the green tops of the leeks and wash the white part carefully. Bring a pan of salted water to the boil and put in the whole leeks. Simmer gently until they are tender, then tip them into a colander to drain thoroughly. Meanwhile, make the dressing. Don't compromise; there should be 5-6 tablespoons olive oil to 1 tablespoon of wine vinegar, a little salt and a little more freshly ground black pepper. Pour this dressing over the leeks while they are still warm, and sprinkle with the chopped onion. Leave the leeks to cool. Just before serving, mix the mayonnaise with the cream, taste for seasoning, and spread this mixture in a thick layer over the leeks. Decorate with finely chopped parsley.

This dish is quite delicious on its own, but if you do have to stretch it, slices of a good garlic sausage or smoked ham and some black olives will go very well with it, and the colours are lovely.

Leeks à la Grecque

This is a general method which can be used for all sorts of vegetables; mushrooms, cauliflower, French and runner beans, Jerusalem artichokes, and even thickly sliced onions.

1 lb leeks	3 peppercorns
½ pint water	2 cloves crushed garlic
2 fl oz olive oil	1 teasp coriander
2 bayleaves	2 tblsps tomato purée
1 teasp salt	Juice of ½ lemon

Put the water, oil, bayleaves, salt, peppercorns, garlic and coriander into a saucepan and bring to a fast boil. Dilute the tomato purée with a little lemon juice and add it to the pan. Simmer for about 10 minutes while preparing the leeks. Trim them of their green leaves, wash the white part thoroughly and cut it into 2″ lengths. Add them to the pan and continue to simmer, uncovered, until the leeks are tender. Allow to cool, then tip carefully into a shallow dish, squeeze the lemon juice over them and serve cold. It is even better made the day before you need it.

Cooked Vegetable Salads

Beetroot Salad

Boil, or bake (this takes longer, but the flavour is better) small beetroot in their skins until tender. Drain, cool and peel. Either slice then, or chop them finely. Dress them with a French dressing (*see* page 125), and garnish with a few caraway seeds. Alternatively, make a dressing from sour cream mixed with a very little red wine vinegar and plenty of freshly-ground black pepper.

Brussels Sprout Salad

Prepare 1 lb small, firm sprouts and cook them until *just* tender. Drain them well, and while they are still warm, fold them into a mustardy French dressing. Add a few chopped walnuts if you have them. French and runner beans can be served in the same way, substituting almonds for walnuts.

Raw Vegetable Salads

Carrot Salad

A carefully made carrot salad is very good as part of a mixed *hors d'oeuvres;* celeriac and parsnips can be prepared in the same way. A vegetable-shredder like the *mouli-juliénne* is very useful here.

Peel the carrots and shred them finely; make a dressing with 6 tablespoons olive oil to one of wine vinegar, salt and freshly-ground pepper, and, in this case, a pinch of sugar. Sprinkle with chopped parsley and a little chopped onion. Make the dressing for celeriac with lemon juice rather than vinegar, to stop it from turning brown.

Chicory Salad with Walnuts and Chicken Livers

'Sugarloaf' chicory (*see* page 24) is very good for this salad; otherwise, use the ordinary blanched kind.

2-3 heads of chicory, separated into leaves	1 tblsp red wine vinegar
	1 dstspn Meaux mustard
1-2 chicken livers	Salt and pepper
6 tblsps olive oil	2 oz walnuts

Chop the chicken livers and fry them in a mixture of oil and butter until very crisp and brown. Drain on kitchen paper. Make a french dressing with the oil and vinegar, mustard, salt and pepper. Stir in the roughly chopped walnuts, and the chicken livers. Fold the chicory into this dressing only just before serving; it makes a very good lunch, served with bread and cheese.

Dried Vegetables

Chick peas, flageolets, haricot beans and green lentils all make delicious salads. Allow 2 oz per person for a first course, 3 oz for a main course. Soak them for about 4 hours beforehand, but if you forget, use the method on page 173. Put the drained beans into a pan and cover with cold water; add a *bouquet garni* and a sliced onion and carrot, but no salt. Simmer gently until tender – green lentils and flageolets will probably only take about 45 minutes, chick peas and haricot beans may need almost 2 hours.

Drain, remove the flavouring herbs and vegetables, and mix with a French dressing, chopped parsley and garlic, and plenty of salt.

For a lunch or supper dish, serve them warm in their garlic flavoured dressing, with bacon strips and sausages. Or fry a chopped onion in some butter and mix this into the beans, with some cubes of ham, or tuna.

Tuna and haricot beans (*tonno e fagioli*) is a favourite Italian lunch dish, and the best version I ever had was in a motorway restaurant – melting beans, plenty of tuna, a good dressing made with plenty of olive oil, and the whole seasoned with chopped fresh basil.

FISH

Salted or smoked fish often feature in mixed *hors d'oeuvres* in France. Tinned sardines and anchovies are the most easily available in this country, but I prefer Norwegian sild or brisling which have a more subtle flavour. Smoked mackerel used to be something of a rarity, and very good. A new process has meant that there is much more of it about, but, as usual, at the expense of quality – the flesh is very oily, and rather pulpy. If you have a fish-smoker, you can make your own. Choose fairly small fish and ask the fishmonger to gut them and remove the heads. Use the normal smokedust, but add some sprigs of thyme and a bayleaf or two, to scent the fish as it smokes. You can smoke sprats and trout in the same way – they make equally good first courses.

Caveach

This method of preserving fish originated in the West Indies (the name comes from the Spanish word for the method, *escabeche*). Popular in this country in the 18th century, it is a delicious way of dealing with herring and mackerel, and should be eaten as a first course with brown bread and butter.

Method: Have the fish filleted, then cut each fillet into pieces roughly 2 in square. Rub into each piece a mixture of grated nutmeg, freshly ground pepper, a little ground cloves and salt (the amounts needed for 6 large herrings would be ½ oz pepper, 1 teasp nutmeg, ½ teasp cloves, 2 oz block salt). Let the fish stand about 4 hours; then fry the pieces, on both sides, until brown. Let them get quite cold, then put them into a clean jar and cover them with vinegar by at least an inch. To keep them for several months, cover the surface of the vinegar with a film of oil. Cover the jar tightly and store in a cool place, where you should leave it for at least a week before eating the fish. It is worth making a quantity at a time, as the pieces can be removed as and when you need them.

Salted Sprats

2 lb sprats, heads and tails removed	2 teasps green peppercorns
12 oz block salt	6 bayleaves
10 black peppercorns	6 juniper berries

Gut the sprats using a sharp knife – it is a fiddly job. Mix the salt, bayleaves, peppercorns and juniper berries. Put a layer of this in a stoneware jar, then a layer of sprats, then more salt, and so on, finishing with a salt and spice layer. Cover the jar with waxed paper, then with foil, and put a weight on top. Brine will soon form as the fish juices melt the salt, and the fish must stay submerged. Although the fish themselves are preserved, the oil they release may go rancid if the larder is not very cool. But they will keep indefinitely in the fridge and are delicious served with hot buckwheat pancakes (make your usual pancake recipe with buckwheat flour in place of ordinary white flour), and lots of sour cream.

MEAT AND FISH PASTES

These make good first courses, and lunch dishes, served with toast and butter. They are also an excellent way of using up leftover meat and game.

Make sure the meat is drained of any juices or gravy. Mince it finely, having first removed gristly pieces; beat in half its weight of butter if it is lean meat, one-third of its weight if you are using a fat piece of beef or ham. Season with salt, pepper and mace or nut-meg. Pack into small pots and seal with clarified butter. It is not necessary to freeze potted meat; simply seal it with clarified butter and store it in the fridge. Once you have broken the butter seal, eat it within 36 hours.

To Clarify Butter

It is worth preparing this in fairly large quantities, as it is very useful for frying fish.

Melt 1 lb butter slowly in a saucepan. Take the pan off the heat as soon as the butter has melted and leave it to stand for 10 minutes. Line a sieve with a piece of paper towel and stand it over a margarine tub (in which you can store the butter). Pour the melted butter through the sieve, and either use it immediately for sealing your meat or fish paste (pour about ½" over the top of the paste), or cover the margarine tub and store it for future use, in the fridge.

Finnan Haddock Paste

1 large, or 2 small, Finnan haddocks	4 oz butter
1 pint milk and water mixed	Freshly-ground pepper
2 bayleaves	Clarified butter to seal

Cover the haddock with the milk and water in a heavy saucepan, add the bayleaves and a little pepper, and poach gently until the fish is cooked. Lift it out and drain very thoroughly. Remove the skin and bones and flake it into a bowl. Add the butter, softened but not melted, and beat until fish and butter are well blended. Season with freshly-ground pepper, and salt if it is necessary. Pack into stoneware jars and seal with clarified butter.

Rillettes

These are the cheapest and easiest of all the French potted meats and are a great standby. They too will keep for sometime sealed with lard. Again, do not freeze.

2 lb belly pork	4 cloves garlic
¼ pint white wine or cider	Black pepper, salt
Sprigs of rosemary	
and thyme	

Remove the rind and any bones from the pork and chop it roughly into cubes. Put it into a shallow ovenproof dish with the wine or cider, the herbs, crushed garlic, salt and pepper. Cook, covered with foil, in a very low oven until the pork is very soft – about 4 hours at 275° F. Tip the pork into a colander set over a basin. Remove the herbs and chop the meat with a *demi-lune* or a very sharp knife; do not blend it in a blender as this produces too smooth a mixture. The charm of this dish is its rough texture. Taste for seasoning and pack into small jars. When the fat on top of the drained juices has set, take it out of the basin, remelt it and use it to seal the jars, adding fresh melted lard if necessary to cover the meat completely. Serve with wholemeal toast and gherkins or green olives.

The pork rinds can be cooked at the same time, in an uncovered cake tin, on a higher shelf. When they are crisp, drain them on kitchen paper. Break them into chunks and sprinkle with salt. Serve them cold with drinks, or give them to the children to take to school for break. In the Black Country they are called 'scratchings' and in France *rillons* – they are unfailingly popular.

Finally, one *pâté* for a special occasion; it is expensive, and hard work, but extremely good.

Duck and Orange Pâté

1 large duck and its liver	2 large sweet oranges
1 lb belly pork,	1 egg
rind and bones removed	Salt, pepper
¾ lb boneless stewing veal	Thyme
3 fl oz white wine	Coriander
1 Seville orange	2 tblsp brandy

Bone the duck, which is a messy task, but not difficult. You need a very sharp short-bladed knife and a firm wooden board. Put the duck breast down and make an incision from top to bottom along the back bone. Holding the skin in one hand, follow the carcase of the bird round with your knife; detach wings and legs by inserting the point of the knife in the joints where they join the body, and levering until they come free. Remove the drumsticks and wingbones from the skin by turning them inside out and sliding your knife along the bones to detach them from the flesh. Use these bones and the carcass for stock. Remove the flesh from the skin, then season the skin with salt, pepper, coriander and thyme.

Cut half the pork, the liver of the duck, and the breast flesh into cubes and mix them with half the white wine, the juice of the Seville orange, salt, pepper and coriander. Leave to stand overnight. Mince the veal, the rest of the duck flesh and the belly pork finely. Stir in the rest of the white wine, the squeezed juice of the two sweet oranges, salt, pepper, a little more thyme, and bind with the beaten egg. Leave this to stand overnight too. Next day, test this forcemeat for seasoning by frying a small piece and allowing it to get quite cold before tasting it. Adjust the seasoning if necessary.

Brown the outside of the duck skin in a frying pan. Arrange a design of whole bayleaves on the bottom of a stoneware terrine, and put the duck skin gently on top, lining the terrine with it. Put in a layer of forcemeat and a layer of cubed meat, and continue like this until both are used up, finishing with a layer of forcemeat. Pour the brandy over, then fold over the skin of the duck, if there is still some showing above the meat. Cover the terrine with foil and a lid and stand it in a baking tin half filled with water. Cook for 2 hours at 310° F, or until the *pâté* has shrunk away from the sides of the terrine. Cool overnight, with two tins on top to act as weights. Next day, run a thick layer of melted lard over the surface, wrap the whole thing in foil and store for at least a week in the bottom of the fridge. Give it at least 1 hour at room temperature before eating. A salad of crisp Florence fennel is very good with it.

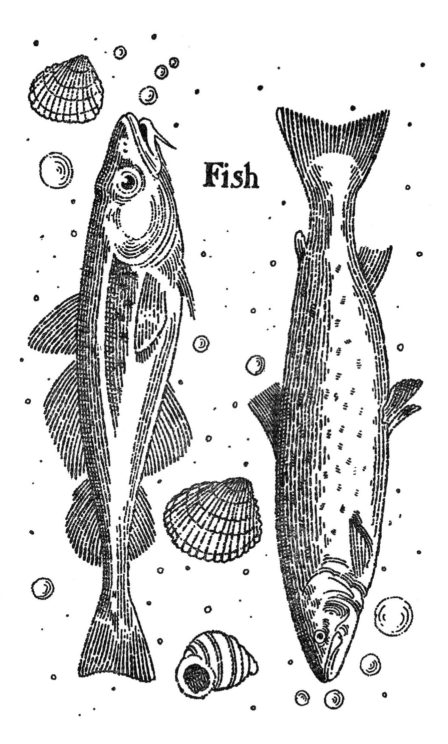

Fish

Fish

I have limited the recipes in this chapter to those which deal with fish most commonly found on fishmongers' slabs. Sadly, the choice in this country is often very limited, except in those areas which boast large immigrant communities. We are even more conservative about fish than we are about vegetables, but while ever more exotic vegetables appear in the shops, thanks to persistent requests for them, the only 'exotic' fish to be seen is an occasional scallop or lobster. But the quality of our fish is often superb, so that even the most humdrum coley is worth cooking with care.

THE OILY FISH: MACKEREL, HERRINGS, SPRATS

Being so rich in oil makes them particularly suitable for grilling, and there is almost nothing better than really fresh grilled mackerel.

Grilled Mackerel

To prepare it, simply gut each fish, reserving any roe. Season the roes with salt, freshly ground black pepper, lemon juice and a little chopped fennel. Return the roes to the bellies of the fish. Score each mackerel three times on each side with a sharp knife, and rub with a little olive oil and salt. Arrange them on the grid of the grill pan, and grill for about 10 minutes on each side. Transfer them to a hot dish, sprinkle with more salt and serve very hot with plenty of lemon wedges (not slices – I immediately downgrade any restaurant which serves me with slices, rather than wedges, of lemon to squeeze over fish; it looks mean, and it is impossible to wring more than a few drops out of them).

Allonby Mackerel

Just up the coast from Allonby, a small village on the Solway coast, it is possible to gather beautiful small black mussels. The beach is quite unpolluted, except by coal, which at low tide stripes the sand with black. The mussels do have a slight coal flavour, which adds to their charm.

4 large mackerel	1 small onion
2 lb mussels	1 clove garlic
½ pint white wine or dry cider	Large bunch parsley
	Salt and pepper

Gut the mackerel and remove the heads. Scrub the mussels and put them in a large pan with the white wine or cider. Boil rapidly, with the lid on, shaking the pan, until all the mussels have opened. Strain the liquor through a sieve lined with muslin into a small jug. Remove the mussels from their shells and mix with the finely chopped onion, garlic and parsley. Season with salt and pepper and stuff the mackerel with this mixture. Any left-over stuffing can be used as a bed for the mackerel; arrange them on it in a shallow greased baking dish. Pour the strained mussel liquor over them and bake for about 35 minutes at 375° F, basting with the juices and adding a little more white wine or cider if necessary. Serve on their own, with any vegetables as a separate course.

Hot Smoked Mackerel with Horseradish Cream

You will need a fish-smoker for this dish.

4 small mackerel	either fresh, or vacuum-packed
½ dozen bayleaves	
Large handful of smokedust	2 teasps wine vinegar
1 oz fresh white breadcrumbs	¼ pint whipping cream
4 oz grated horseradish,	Salt and pepper

Arrange the smokedust and the bayleaves in the bottom of the smoker; sprinkle the mackerel (gutted but otherwise whole) with a little salt and put them on the grid, head to tail. Put the lid on the smoker, light the pan of methylated spirits and leave the fish to smoke while you prepare the sauce. Mix the breadcrumbs with the horseradish and vinegar. Whip the cream according to the instructions on the tub, then fold in the horseradish mixture. Add salt and freshly-ground pepper to taste. Keep this sauce in the fridge until the fish is ready, then serve with it.

Cold Mackerel with Salsa Verde

4 mackerel	*Bouquet garni* of fennel,
¼ pint white wine	parsley stalks, thyme and
2 tblsps white wine vinegar	lemon peel
6 peppercorns	Salt

Put about 1½ pints water into a large pan and add all the other ingredients except the fish; bring to the boil, then reduce the temperature and simmer gently for about 20 minutes. Gut the mackerel and remove the heads and tails. Lower them gently into the simmering *court-bouillon*, and poach gently for 15 minutes. Leave them to cool in the liquid. Lift them out and fillet them carefully, arranging them on a flat plate. Make the sauce, which is basically a *vinaigrette*:

Large bunch parsley	1 teasp green peppercorns
Small bunch watercress	2 tblsps white wine vinegar
1 teasp capers	Salt and pepper
1 pickled cucumber	¼ pint olive oil
1 dstspn finely chopped onion	

Remove the stalks from the parsley and watercress and chop them, the capers, pickled cucumber (or gherkins) and the onion almost to a purée. Stir in the crushed green peppercorns, the vinegar and salt, then, gradually, the oil. Check the seasoning and serve with the fish.

Baked Herrings with Red Wine Sauce

4 large herrings
½ pint red wine
Salt and pepper
2 cloves

1 sliced onion
1 oz butter
1 tblsp flour

Scale and gut the herrings. Most good fishmongers will automatically scale herrings. Otherwise, hold the fish firmly by the tail and scrape towards the head with the back of a knife. Best done in the sink as the scales fly about. Grease an ovenproof dish and arrange the fish in it, head to tail. Bring to the boil, in a small pan, the wine, salt and pepper, cloves and onion; pour it over the fish, cover with butter papers and bake for 35 minutes at 350° F, or until the fish is done. Transfer the fish to a hot plate, work the flour into the butter and add this, in small pieces, to the simmering sauce, stirring constantly until the sauce is thick. Check the seasoning – it should be fairly spicy – pour into a sauceboat and serve with the fish.

Mustard Grilled Herrings

4 herrings, scaled, gutted,
    and heads removed
2 tblsps Meaux mustard

Potato purée
Chopped parsley

Make two incisions with a sharp knife on both sides of each herring. Rub mustard into these incisions and put a little inside each fish. Grill under a hot grill for about 10 minutes on each side. Serve on a bed of prepared potato purée – floury potatoes put through a vegetable-mill with plenty of hot milk, butter, salt, freshly-ground pepper and nutmeg, accompanied by a bowl of chopped parsley.

Sprats with Bacon, Parsley and Garlic

1½ lb sprats
4 oz medium oatmeal,
    seasoned
4 rashers streaky bacon

2 cloves chopped garlic
5 tblsps chopped parsley
2 quartered lemons

Gut the sprats (a fiddly job – the small ones can be left whole) and roll them in the seasoned oatmeal. Cut the bacon into strips. Divide the sprats and bacon into batches according to the size of your frying pan. Have a large meat dish ready in a warm oven. Melt a very little dripping in the frying pan and fry one batch of fish and bacon at a time, both should be crisp and golden. It will take about 12 minutes over a medium heat, turning the fish once. Transfer each batch to the warm dish as it is ready. Mix the chopped garlic and parsley and sprinkle this over the pile of sprats and bacon; surround it with the lemon quarters and serve very hot.

Sprats can be smoked in the same way as the mackerel on page 63 and served hot, with a jar of good Dijon or Meaux mustard.

WHITE FISH

A great many of the most delicious and delicate fish come under this rather inelegant heading, but here I am going to concentrate on cod, coley and haddock.

Chowder

A most comforting and easily-made dish.

2 large onions	2 bayleaves
8 oz streaky bacon	Salt, freshly ground pepper
or salt belly pork	3 tblsps double cream
3 large potatoes	Chopped parsley
1 lb coley	Fried bread
1 pint milk	

Cut the onion into slices and the bacon or pork into cubes. Put the bacon in a heavy casserole over a gentle heat until the fat runs, then add the onion, cover the pan and continue to cook gently until the onion is transparent. Meanwhile, peel and slice the potatoes and cut the fish into cubes, heat the milk and infuse the bayleaves in it. When the onion is ready, put alternate layers of potato and fish on top, ending with a layer of potato. Pour the milk over all, add salt and pepper and simmer very gently until the potato is done – about 40 minutes. Stir in the cream, sprinkle with parsley and serve with pieces of bread fried crisp in olive oil.

'Mediterranean' Fish Stew

6 oz prawns, in their shells
1½ lb cockles or mussels
2 large onions
4 cloves garlic
4 tblsps olive oil
2 15 oz cans Italian tomatoes
Bouquet garni of thyme,

parsley, fennel and
orange peel
¼ pint white wine
½ pint fish stock (see method)
1 lb squid
1 lb cod
Salt and pepper

First, make the fish stock. Shell the prawns and cover the shells with ½ pint cold water. Bring to the boil and simmer for about 20 minutes. Scrub the mussels or cockles. Strain the prawn stock into a large pan, put in the mussels or cockles and cook over a high heat, with the lid on, until all the shells are open. Remove the fish and strain the stock through muslin into a jug or bowl.

Melt the sliced onions and garlic in the olive oil until soft. Add the tomatoes, bouquet garni and white wine and strained stock; bring to the boil, lower the heat and simmer for 10 minutes. Clean the squid – turn them inside out and pull out the intestines and the transparent blade – the tentacles will come too. Throw away the intestines, but chop the tentacles and the body of the squid into pieces. Add these to the tomatoes in the pan and cook very gently until they are tender (about 40 minutes to one hour). Then add the cockles or mussels, the cod and the prawns. Cook very gently for a further 10 minutes. Taste for seasoning, remove the herbs and serve with saffron rice.

Fish Cakes

1 lb smooth mashed potato
1 lb cooked white fish
4 oz garlic cream cheese
    (Boursin, or home-made)
Chopped parsley

Salt and pepper
Seasoned flour
Beaten egg
Breadcrumbs

Mix the potato, fish and cream cheese thoroughly, then add the parsley; if the mixture seems too dry, add more cream cheese. Check the seasoning. Form into small flat cakes and roll in seasoned flour. Dip in the beaten egg, then in the breadcrumbs, and arrange them on a cake rack to dry for 15 minutes. Fry in hot olive oil for about 10 minutes on each side.

Shrimp and Cod Pancakes

8 oz cod
8 oz shelled shrimps
¾ pint milk
¼ pint double cream
1 bayleaf

Salt, pepper
2 oz butter
2 oz flour
2 teasps anchovy essence

Cook the cod gently in the milk with a little salt and pepper and the bayleaf. Lift out the cod with a fish slice and flake into a bowl; stir in the shrimps. Melt the butter and stir in the flour. Off the heat, add the milk gradually until you have a smooth sauce; return it to the heat and bring the sauce to the boil, stirring constantly. Simmer very gently for a further 20 minutes. Stir the cod, shrimps and anchovy essence into the sauce and check the seasoning. It will be easier to fill the pancakes with this mixture if you leave it to cool overnight. Make the pancakes according to your usual recipe and method and put 2 tablespoons of the filling into each one. Roll it up and arrange in a buttered fireproof dish. Pour the cream over the pancakes, season with a little salt and black pepper and heat in a 375° F oven until golden brown and bubbling.

Cold Fried Fish with Tarator Sauce

1½ lb haddock fillet
Salt and black pepper
Lemon juice
1-2 cloves crushed garlic

Seasoned flour
Beaten egg
Breadcrumbs
Olive oil

Skin the fillets and remove any bones; cut into large pieces and season each piece with salt, pepper, lemon juice and crushed garlic. Leave the fish to stand for an hour or two. Dip the pieces in seasoned flour, then in the egg, then in the breadcrumbs. Fry in hot olive oil until golden brown and firm – about 8-10 minutes on each side. Drain on kitchen paper, then leave to get quite cold. Properly fried and drained, it will remain crisp.

Tarator Sauce

I first tasted this sauce in the Lebanon, served not with fish, but with a very scrawny chicken spit-roasted over an open fire. The chicken was tough but the flavour wonderful, and we finished the sauce with bread. Pine nuts should be used, but ground almonds make a very good substitute.

2 slices good white bread, with the crusts removed
A little fish stock, if available
8 oz ground almonds, or pine nuts

Juice of 1 large or 2 small lemons
2 crushed cloves garlic
Salt

Soak the bread in the cold stock (or water), then squeeze it hard. Put it in the blender, add the ground almonds, lemon juice, garlic and salt. Blend to a smooth paste. Decorate it and the fish with black olives and parsley.

PRESERVED FISH

Smoked Haddock Soufflé

¾ lb smoked haddock
¼ pint milk
2 oz butter
2 oz flour
2 egg yolks

2 oz Gruyère
2 tblsps double cream
3 egg whites
1 tblsp breadcrumbs

Preheat the oven to 375° F.

Cook the haddock in the milk. Remove the fish and flake it. Melt the butter, stir in the flour, and add the milk slowly, stirring constantly. Bring to the boil, still stirring then simmer for 10 minutes; remove the sauce from the heat and beat in the egg yolks, one at a time. Fold in the fish and most of the cheese, grated. Add the cream and taste for seasoning. Butter a soufflé dish. Whip the egg whites stiffly and fold into the soufflé base with a metal spoon. Pour into the prepared dish, sprinkle with the remaining cheese, and the breadcrumbs and bake until well risen – about 25 minutes.

Smoked Haddock Flan

8 oz shortcrust pastry	2 eggs
1 large Finnan haddock	¼ pint thin cream
1 tblsp chopped chervil	Salt and pepper

Line a flan tin with the pastry. Prick the base, fit in a piece of foil, pressing it well down, and bake blind at 425° F for 15 minutes. Remove the foil and return the flan case to the oven for a further 10 minutes to set the base. Take it out, leave it to cool a little, and lower the oven temperature to 375° F.

Cook the haddock in a little milk and water; remove the skin and bones and mix it with the chopped chervil, then spread it in the flan case. Beat the eggs with the cream and season them with salt and freshly ground black pepper – pour over the fish. Put the flan on to a baking sheet and bake for 30 minutes. Eat the flan warm, rather than hot. It is also good cold if eaten within 24 hours.

Breakfast Kippers

1 real kipper (from the Isle of Man, Craster or Loch Fyne) per person	Unsalted butter Black pepper Wholemeal toast

Put the whole kippers head first into a tall jug, with only their tails showing over the top. Pour in very hot water, up to the brim. Leave them for 10 minutes and preheat the grill. Cover the grill pan grid with foil. Put the drained kippers on this, flesh side uppermost, and slide them under the grill, with a large lump of unsalted butter on each, for 5 minutes. Serve them with plenty of freshly-ground black pepper and wholemeal toast. The foil makes washing up the grill pan much easier.

Kippers and Lentils

1 packet frozen kipper fillets   1 small onion
6 oz green lentils   Parsley
French dressing made with
    lemon juice

Defrost the kipper fillets. Prepare the lentils according to the method on page 173; at the end of the soaking time, drain them, and return them to the pan with fresh water, a bayleaf, sliced onion and carrot – no salt. Simmer until done, which depends on the age of the lentils; 45 minutes to an hour should be enough. Drain well, remove the vegetables and dress with the French dressing while still warm, together with the finely chopped onion and parsley. Slice the raw kippers very thinly, and mix into the salad. Serve slightly chilled, with extra lemon juice to taste.

SHELLFISH

For the reasons I mentioned at the beginning of the chapter, I have limited the recipes in this section to the most easily available shellfish. I would say, too, that frozen shellfish are not worth buying – the freezing process seems to make them tough and tasteless. One of the nastiest products of the freezer in recent years is frozen scampi; compare them with fresh Dublin Bay prawns when you can get them and you will see what I mean.

Scallops and Bacon

Shellfish and bacon have a special affinity, and this recipe works well with mussels and cockles too.

6-8 scallops   Salt and pepper
4 rashers bacon   Chopped parsley
Butter   A little white wine

If the scallops are still tightly shut, put them in a pan with about $\frac{1}{2}''$ water and steam them over a high heat until they open. Slice the white part and keep the corals whole – discard everything else. Chop the bacon and cook it until transparent in about 2 oz butter. Add the sliced white part of the scallops and cook over a medium heat, turning frequently with a metal spoon. Add the corals, and cook for a further 5 minutes, until they lose their raw look. Sprinkle a little salt, plenty of freshly ground pepper, and a generous tablespoonful of chopped parsley over the shellfish and stir again before tipping them onto a hot plate. Pour a wine-glassful of white wine into the pan and bring it to the boil, stirring in any residue, and reducing it by about half. Pour this over the waiting scallops and bacon, and serve with garlic bread, or a pile of buttery rice.

Shellfish Risotto

4 oz unshelled prawns	4 oz butter
2 lb fresh mussels	1 large onion
1 lb fresh cockles	1 stick celery
4 oz peeled shrimps	2 cloves garlic
About 2½ pints stock	12 oz Italian rice
(see method)	A little paprika
½ pint white wine	Salt and pepper

Shell the prawns, cover the shells with 1½ pints water and simmer for half-an-hour. Strain and use this liquor to open the shells of the scrubbed cockles and mussels. Strain again, this time through muslin into a measuring jug, add the white wine and make the quantity up to 2½ pints with water if necessary. Melt the butter in a heavy pan and cook the finely chopped onion, celery and garlic until transparent. Stir in the rice and mix thoroughly until every grain of rice is coated with butter. Pour the stock into a saucepan and keep it hot over a low heat while you cook the rice – pour in enough to cover the rice and simmer over a medium heat until the rice has absorbed the stock. Add more hot stock to cover the rice and simmer until it has been absorbed; continue to add stock in this way until the rice is tender but still has a bite to it. Add the cockles and mussels, the shrimps and prawns, and mix thoroughly with the rice, together with paprika, salt and freshly-ground pepper. Serve with Parmesan, freshly grated if possible.

Mussels with 'Snail' Butter

3 lb large mussels
4 oz butter
2 cloves finely chopped
   garlic

2 tblsps finely chopped
   parsley and tarragon
Salt and pepper
A little lemon juice

Work the butter with the garlic, herbs, freshly-ground pepper, a little salt and a squeeze of lemon juice. Open the mussels in the usual way and discard the top shells, leaving each mussel in the bottom half of its shell. Put a teaspoon of the snail butter into each, arrange in one layer in a large baking tin and put into a hot oven for long enough to melt butter, but not too long or the mussels will toughen – 10 minutes should be ample. Provide plenty of good bread to mop up the butter, and lots of cold dry white wine.

Shellfish Croûtes

8 oz assorted cooked shellfish :
   cockles, mussels, chopped
   scallops, shrimps, prawns,
   crab, all, or any, of these
2 tblsps white wine
4 tblsps thick cream

4 large slices of good white
   bread, crusts removed
1-2 oz butter and 1 tblsp olive
   oil
Salt, freshly ground pepper
Chopped watercress

Heat the white wine in a small saucepan, add the shellfish, and stir well; pour in the cream and let all bubble gently while you fry the bread in the butter and oil until golden and crisp. Put each piece of fried bread on a warm plate, season the shellfish with salt and freshly ground pepper and pile some of this mixture on top of each piece of bread. Sprinkle with chopped watercress and serve immediately, before the bread can go soggy.

Cockle and Leek Pie

3 lb cockles, in their shells   2 oz flour
2 oz butter   ¾ pint stock *(see recipe)*
3 rashers bacon   Salt and black pepper
4 leeks   8 oz shortcrust pastry

Wash the cockles, and open them in about ½ pint water. Strain the
liquor carefully into a measuring jug – cockles are often very sandy
– there should be about ¾ pint; if there is more, reduce it to that
amount by fast boiling. Rinse the shelled cockles in a colander and
leave them to drain. Melt the butter and add the bacon, cut into
strips, and the finely sliced leeks. Leave them to cook gently until
the leeks are soft. Off the heat, stir in the flour, and add the stock
slowly, stirring continuously until you have a smooth sauce. Return
it to the heat and bring it to the boil, then simmer for about 5
minutes before adding the cockles. Season with salt and black pepper. Pour into a pie dish, fit a strip of pastry round the rim, then
pinch the pastry lid on to this; make a hole in the middle, decorate
the top and brush with a little beaten egg. Bake at 375° F until the
pastry is crisp and pale gold – about 35-40 minutes.

FRESHWATER FISH: SALMON, SALMON TROUT, TROUT AND CHAR

Simple and unpretentious recipes are best if you are lucky enough
to procure these fish in prime condition.

To Cook Salmon and Salmon Trout

I think the foil method of cooking both is best, even if you do
possess a fish-kettle. A large fish looks far better straight than curved
round on itself, as well as being easier to serve.

   1) If the fish is to be eaten hot, brush the foil with melted butter;
if cold, with oil. Otherwise you will have an unappetizing crust of
cold butter to spoil the appearance of the fish.

   2) Season the foil, as well as the fish. Add a very few flavouring

herbs – chervil, fennel or tarragon – but if the fish is really fresh even these aren't necessary.

3) Fold the edges of the foil together carefully, to seal all the juices inside – don't wrap it too tightly round the fish.

4) Bake at 300° F for 1¼ hours for a large piece of salmon, or a whole fish weighing up to 6 lb. Over that weight, add another 15 minutes for each pound.

5) Cool fish to be eaten cold in its parcel; if you are serving it for lunch, cook it the evening before; for dinner, cook it early in the morning.

6) Fish to be eaten hot should rest for 5-10 minutes in the foil before serving.

7) A *beurre blanc* is the best possible sauce to serve with hot salmon or sea-trout.

Beurre Blanc

There is a myth that this is a difficult sauce to make, but it is far easier than an *hollandaise* as it contains no eggs, and only calls for an uninterrupted 10 minutes in which to make it.

1 small mild onion	4 tblsps white wine vinegar
4 tblsps white wine	8 oz unsalted butter

Chop the onion extremely finely and put it into a small saucepan with the wine and vinegar. Simmer, uncovered, until the onion is soft and the wine and vinegar mostly absorbed. Tip the contents of the pan into a basin which will fit over a saucepan or a *bain-marie* if you have one, and leave it until you are ready to make the sauce. Cut the butter into cubes and keep it in the fridge until needed. About 10 minutes before you are ready to eat, pour hot water into the saucepan, stand the basin over it and put the saucepan over a very low heat. When the onion is hot, start adding the butter, 2-3 cubes at a time, whisking with a balloon whisk or fork as it softens; continue to add butter and whisk until all the butter has been used up, and you have a light, creamy sauce. Making the sauce over hot water minimises the risk of ending up simply with melted butter. Season the *beurre blanc* with a little salt and pepper and serve it immediately. It is delicious not only with salmon, but also with trout, turbot, any grilled white fish, and even with lobster.

Sauce Quimper

Another delicious and simple sauce, this time for cold fish. It is served with mackerel in Brittany, but I find it too rich for such fish; it seems to work better with trout, salmon-trout and char.

2 egg yolks
1 teasp Dijon or Meaux
    mustard
Salt, pepper
1 teasp white wine vinegar
2 tblsps of whatever fresh

herbs are available –
parsley, chervil, tarragon,
chives, fennel – finely
chopped
3 oz melted butter

Stir the mustard, salt, pepper, vinegar and chopped herbs into the raw egg yolks. Melt the butter gently and let it cool a little before adding it gradually to the eggs, stirring constantly. Check the seasoning and serve it in a sauce boat, as it is fairly liquid.

Cold Trout with Sauce Quimper

For 4 trout, prepare a *court-bouillon* :

3 pints water
¼ pint white wine
Large bunch herbs

3 tblsps white wine vinegar
1 tblsp salt
6 peppercorns

Boil all the ingredients together for about 10 minutes, then slip in the gutted trout. Simmer very gently for 10 minutes, then leave the fish to cool in the liquid. Serve them cold with *Sauce Quimper* (see above). Very fresh trout can be cooked as above (*au bleu*), and then eaten hot with the *beurre blanc*.

Trout with Nuts

A variation of trout with almonds.

4 fat trout
8 oz almonds and hazel nuts
Seasoned flour
1 beaten egg

Clarified butter
3 oz butter
Chopped fresh tarragon
Lemon quarters

Put the nuts into the blender and chop them, but stop before they become a powder. Gut the trout and sprinkle them with seasoned flour; dip them in the beaten egg then roll them in the chopped nuts until they are well-coated. Heat the clarified butter in a large frying pan and fry the trout in it over a medium heat, turning once, for 10 minutes on each side. Be careful that the nuts do not burn. Melt the 3 oz of butter in a separate pan, stir in the chopped tarragon, then pour this into a sauce-boat. Transfer the trout carefully to a warm dish, surround them with quarters of lemon and serve with the melted tarragon butter.

Trout with Bacon

This is a Welsh recipe which, provided the bacon is home-cured, gives a delicate flavour to rather flavourless 'battery' reared trout.

4 trout, gutted
Salt, freshly ground pepper
Chopped parsley and thyme

About 6 rashers home-cured bacon

Line an ovenproof dish with the bacon – cut each rasher in half if they are long. Season the trout, inside and out, with salt, pepper and the chopped herbs, and lay them on the bacon. Cover with the rest of the rashers and cook for half-an-hour at about 350° F. If the trout are small, 20 minutes should be enough.

Char

As difficult to buy as it is to catch, char is found in the deepest lakes of Northern Europe and was at one time such a common delicacy in the Lake District that special shallow dishes were manufactured for potted char. When you do manage to buy (or catch) any, cook it in any of the ways recommended for trout, which it resembles in size, texture and flavour.

To Pot Char or Trouts

'Clean your Fish well and bone them; wash them with Vinegar, and cut off the Tails, Fins and Heads; season them with Pepper, Salt, Nutmeg and Cloves; then put them close in a Pot, and bake them with a little Verjuice and some Butter; cover them close, let them bake two hours; then pour off the Liquor, and cover them with clarified Butter.' Richard Bradley, *The Country Housewife*, 1753.

Meat

Meat

A good relationship with a good butcher is a valuable asset, especially if you are buying an expensive cut, as so much depends on its having been properly hung. On the other hand, for cheap cuts, you will do just as well to shop around. Another 15p per pound on scrag-end paid to an expensive butcher is not going to make it anything but tough meat which needs slow cooking, while extra money spent on a piece of sirloin from a high-class butcher means you will probably end up with a superlative piece of meat.

BEEF

Castlegate Fillet of Beef

A dish for a special occasion, but not as extravagant as it sounds because there is no waste.

2½ lb fillet of beef,
   well-hung
A large piece of beef fat
½ pint red wine

4 oz butter
½ clove garlic
1 tblsp green peppercorns
Salt, pepper

Grind black pepper over the beef, put the piece of fat on top of the joint, to baste it as it cooks, and roast at 400° F for 15 minutes to the pound, adding the wine to the roasting tin about half way through the cooking time. Baste the meat with this as it mixes with the dripping. Blend the butter with the garlic and the green peppercorns, adding salt if you are using unsalted butter. Shape it into a block and put it in the fridge, well wrapped, until needed. When the beef is cooked, remove the piece of basting fat and transfer the meat to a warm dish; return it to the switched-off oven while you make a gravy from the pan juices – do not thicken them; season with salt and add a little more red wine if necessary. Carve the beef into ½″ thick slices, stopping about three-quarters of the way through the joint, so that you have a sort of toast-rack effect. Slip a slice of the green peppercorn butter between each slice of beef; any butter left over can be left to melt on the dish surrounding the meat. Serve with a potato purée, and follow it with a green salad.

To Stew Beef

'Cut four Pounds of Briscuit, with some of the hard Fat into Pieces; put these into a Pan with some Salt and whole Pepper, and a few Cloves, powdered, and three Quarts of Water, cover the Pan close, and let it stew two Hours; then put some Turnips cut in Dice, a Carrot cut in same manner, the White of a large Leek, two Heads of Sellery shred, and a large Crust of Bread burnt; let it stew an Hour, and serve it.' Richard Bradley, *The Country Housewife*, 1753.

With one or two alterations, this is a very good way of cooking brisket, and it is worth cooking 3 or 4 pounds at a time as it is also delicious cold. I omit the burnt bread (was it to thicken and darken the gravy?), but add two whole onions at the start, and substitute ½ pint brown ale for some of the water. I also make it the day before, so that the fat can be skimmed off before reheating and serving. One celery heart is ample, as I imagine that 20th century celery is probably an altogether larger breed.

A Daube of Beef

1½ lb shoulder steak
½ lb shin – lean and
    not too sinewy
½ lb salt pork
4 cloves garlic
3 large carrots
2 large onions
4 oz green olives

Salt and pepper
2 tblsps tomato purée
Herbs – celery leaves, thyme,
    parsley, bayleaf, strip of
    orange peel
½ pint red wine
A large piece of pork rind

Cut the salt pork and the shin into cubes, and the shoulder steak into wide strips. Put the pork at the bottom of the casserole, then the shoulder steak, then the shin on top of that. Flatten the cloves of garlic with a knife and bury them amongst the beef. Cover the top layer of meat with the sliced carrots and onions, and the olives, drained of their brine, if any. Add a generous amount of salt and freshly ground pepper. Dilute the tomato purée with a little water and pour it in; tie the herbs and orange peel with string and push them deep into the pot. Heat the wine in a small pan and set it alight; when the flames have died down pour it over the contents of the casserole. Lay the piece of pork rind over the top, fat side down; cover that with foil, then fit on the lid of the casserole. Cook for 3½-4 hours at 250° F. When cooked, leave it overnight without removing the lid. Next day, skim off the fat and cut the rind into small squares; stir these into the daube and reheat gently. Check the seasoning and serve with buttered noodles.

Roast Wing Rib of Beef with Yorkshire Pudding and Marrow Bones

This is a combination of the traditional method of roasting meat *over* the pudding, so it catches the juices, and Eliza Acton's recipe for marrow bones baked in batter, dated 1845.

3-4 lb wing rib, on the bone	3 large eggs
6 marrow bones	6 oz plain flour
3 tblsps good dripping	Salt and pepper
¾ pint milk	

Preheat the oven to 425° F. Stand the beef on a grid over the roasting tin, smear the top surface with the dripping, and grind pepper over it. Put it to roast for half-an-hour. Make a batter with the milk, eggs, flour, a pinch of salt and some black pepper. Take the meat out of the oven and put the marrow bones into the tin. Pour the Yorkshire pudding batter over them and return everything to the oven for a further ¾ of an hour, or until the pudding is well-risen and golden brown, and the meat tender. If the meat is ready before the pudding, transfer it to a warm dish and keep it warm; it will be more tender, and easier to carve. Give each person a teaspoon to scoop out the marrow on to slices of beef. The pudding will be full of beef juice, so no extra gravy is really necessary.

Salt Beef and Trotters

A substantial dish in which the pigs' trotters add richness to the silverside, which can be a rather dry joint.

3 lb silverside of beef, salted for a week to 10 days, either by yourself (page 10), or by the butcher

3 pigs' trotters, split

2 large onions, each stuck with 2 cloves

A sprig of herbs – thyme, parsley stalks, celery leaves, 2 bayleaves, and the green leaves from a leek

A tumbler of brown ale

6 large carrots

Put the beef in a large saucepan, cover it with cold water and bring it to the boil; boil for a minute or two, then throw this water away and replace it with more cold water. Add the scrubbed trotters, the onions, herbs and ale. Bring slowly to the boil once more, then simmer gently for 1½ hours. Scrape the carrots, leave them whole, and add them to the pan; continue cooking slowly, for another ¾ of an hour. Lift the trotters out and let them drain and cool for another dish (*see below*). Leave the beef in its pan for 10 minutes before dishing it up on a warm plate, with the carrots around it. Serve it with parsley dumplings, or floury potatoes boiled in their skins. I like strong English mustard with this dish, rather than horseradish.

Parsley Dumplings

2 oz plain flour

1 tblsp chopped parsley

Pinch baking powder

2 oz fresh white breadcrumbs

2 oz suet

½ teasp salt

Freshly ground pepper

Mix all the dry ingredients together and add enough water to make a soft dough. Roll into small balls the size of a walnut. Have ready a separate large pan containing some of the beef broth (add a little water if necessary) at a rolling boil. Drop in the dumplings, cover tightly and boil for 20 minutes without lifting the lid. Lift them out with a draining spoon and arrange with the carrots round the beef.

Grilled Trotters

A very good first course before something light. Dip the cold cooked trotters into beaten egg, mixed with a generous teaspoon of English mustard, then roll them in seasoned breadcrumbs. Grill first under a medium heat for 20 minutes, turning them often, to ensure that the trotters themselves heat through; then under full heat until the breadcrumbs form a crisp golden crust. Serve quickly on very hot plates with a vinaigrette sauce to which you have added 1 tablespoon chopped capers or gherkins.

Cold Salt Beef with Roman Sauce

A curious and interesting sauce, supposed to have been invented by Apicius.

6 oz stoned dates	1 tblsp clear honey
2 oz blanched almonds	1 tblsp red wine vinegar
1 onion	2 tblsps olive oil
2 tblsps parsley	Salt and pepper

Chop the dates, almonds, onions and parsley very finely, almost to a purée. Stir in the honey and vinegar, then add the oil, gradually. Season with salt and black pepper. Either serve the sauce separately in a bowl, or cover slices of the cold beef with it, arranging them on a plate. This makes a good buffet dish, provided the meat is tender enough to cut with the edge of a fork.

Oxtail with Celeriac Purée

Choose a good thick tail, with plenty of meat in proportion to bone. Trim off excess fat.

1 large oxtail,
    sawn into pieces
1 oz beef dripping
2 large onions
1 oz flour
Pinch ground cloves

2 tblsps Worcester sauce
Salt, pepper
3 bayleaves
2 large carrots
½ pint Guinness
1 large celeriac

Melt the dripping in a frying-pan and brown the pieces of oxtail and
the sliced onions together. Transfer them to a stoneware casserole;
stir the flour into the fat remaining in the pan and add enough hot
water to make a thin gravy. Season with ground cloves, Worcester
sauce, salt, and plenty of freshly-ground black pepper. Bury the bayleaves amongst the oxtail and onions; peel and slice the carrots and
put them in a layer over the meat, then pour the pan gravy over the
top, followed by the Guinness. Cover with a butter paper, foil and
the casserole lid and cook in a 275° F oven for about 3½ hours, or
until the meat is very tender. Leave it until next day, so that you can
remove the thick layer of fat on top. Reheat it gently. Peel the
celeriac and cut into cubes. Cook it in boiling salted water until
tender. Put it through the vegetable-mill, then beat in a generous
lump of butter, a little salt, black pepper and nutmeg. Have plenty
of floury potatoes, boiled in their skins, to soak up the rich oxtail
juices. A wonderful dish for a cold day.

VEAL

Leg of Veal Pot-roasted with Rosemary and Thyme

1 leg of veal – about 3½ lb
3 oz butter
1 tblsp olive oil
1 sprig rosemary

3 sprigs thyme
1 strip lemon peel, chopped
1 large glass white wine
Salt and black pepper

Season the veal, and brown it all over in the butter and oil. Add the
herbs, lemon peel and wine, put a lid on the pan and braise gently
for 2 hours, or until the meat is very tender, basting frequently. Dish

the veal on to a hot plate and taste the pan juices for seasoning before straining them into a gravy boat. Green peas, or young French beans go well with this.

Vitello Tonnato

It is worth cooking more veal than you need for one meal by the above method, so that you have enough left over to make an abbreviated version of this dish.

Slices of cold veal for 4   Lemon juice
Anchovies   Salt and pepper
Capers   Olive oil
Lemon slices   1 small tin of tuna, drained
3 egg yolks   Veal gravy

Make a mayonnise with the egg yolks, lemon juice, salt and pepper and olive oil. Blend in the tuna to make a fairly smooth sauce, then thin it to pouring consistency with the veal gravy. Arrange the slices of veal on a dish and pour the tuna sauce over them. Decorate with capers and anchovies and leave, covered, in a cool place for several hours. Add the lemon slices to the decoration and serve with a cos lettuce salad.

Veal Goulash

2 lb boneless stewing veal   1 pint veal stock
  (shoulder is good)   (made from the shoulder
4 onions   bone)
2 oz butter   2 bayleaves
1 tblsp caraway seeds   Salt and pepper
1 lb tomatoes – tinned   4 tblsps sweet paprika
  have most flavour   ¼ pint sour cream

Cut the veal into cubes and slice 3 of the onions. Brown both in the butter, with the caraway seeds. Skin and chop the tomatoes, if fresh, and add them to the meat. Simmer briskly, then add the stock, bayleaves, salt and pepper. Cover and simmer very gently until the veal is tender – about 2½ hours (I prefer to cook it in a low oven). Slice the last onion and cook it gently in a little butter until transparent but still crisp. Stir it, the paprika and sour cream into the goulash, check the seasoning and reheat without boiling. Serve it with the following dish.

Rice with Green Peppers

2 green peppers	8 oz long-grain rice
1 small onion	Strip lemon peel
2 tblsps olive oil	Salt and pepper

Remove the seeds and white pith from the peppers and slice them into thick strips. Slice the onion. Heat the oil in a pan and cook the onions and peppers in it gently for about 25 minutes, or until the peppers are soft. Tip the rice into a sieve and rinse it under a fast-running cold tap until the water runs clear. Bring a large pan of salted water to the boil, throw in the rice and the lemon peel, stir, let the water return to the boil and time the rice for exactly 12 minutes, with a lid on the pan. Drain well and return to the pan over a gentle heat; stir in the peppers and onions and season well with salt and freshly-ground pepper.

Veal Chops with Juniper and Gin

4 veal chops	1 tblsp juniper berries
2 oz butter	3 tlbsps gin
Salt and pepper	¼ pint double cream

Brown the chops in the butter, season them with salt, pepper and the crushed juniper berries. Cover the pan and cook gently, turning the chops once or twice. They will take about 25-30 minutes to cook, depending on how thick they are. When they are done, remove them to a warm dish and add the gin to the pan juices. When it is hot, set it alight, tipping the pan so that the flames spread. When they have died down, pour in the cream and boil fast until it thickens. Taste for seasoning and pour this sauce over the chops.

Calves' Tongues

These will need about 5 days in brine before cooking. Allow 1-2 per person.

Put them in a large saucepan with 2 carrots, 2 onions and a *bouquet garni*. Add a glass of dry cider, then enough cold water to cover. Bring slowly to the boil, skim, then simmer gently for 2 hours. Skin the tongues while they are still warm, and trim them of any gristle. You can eat them hot with a caper sauce, or use them as part of a *bollito misto* (*see* page 100), cooking them with the other meats.

The following recipe is based on several 18th and 19th century recipes for similar dishes.

Tongue and Sweetbread Pie

2 calves' tongues, cooked as above	4 oz button mushrooms
1 lb calves' sweetbreads	Parsley
Stock (*see method*)	Peel of ½ a lemon
1 oz butter	Salt and black pepper
1 oz flour	6 oz puff pastry

Prepare the sweetbreads: soak them in a bowl of salted water for at least 2 hours (longer if they are frozen). Remove any extraneous pieces of gristle and put them in a pan. Cover them with a combination of white wine, or dry cider, and water. Bring slowly to the boil, then simmer for about 10 minutes, or until they look opaque. Strain their stock into a jug and press the sweetbreads between two plates until cold. Make a sauce with ½ pint sweetbread stock, the butter and flour. Simmer gently while you wipe the mushrooms and blanch them for 5 minutes in boiling salted water to which you have added a squeeze of lemon juice. Drain them well and add them to the sauce. Cut the sweetbreads and tongues into neat pieces and stir them into the sauce too. Chop the parsley and lemon peel finely and season the sauce with them, as well as salt and black pepper. Put a lid on the pan and leave while you roll out the pastry: edge the pie-dish with a strip of pastry, pour in the filling, then pinch the lid onto the strip with damp fingers. Make a hole in the top and decorate, glazing with a little beaten egg. Stand the dish on a baking sheet and cook for 15 minutes at 425° F, before lowering the heat to 400° F for a further 20 minutes.

LAMB

Boiled Shoulder of Lamb

The success of this dish lies in very slow simmering.

1 whole shoulder lamb	3 onions, each stuck with a clove
1 parsnip	4 sprigs thyme
2 carrots	8 black peppercorns
½ turnip	Salt

Scrub the parsnip, carrots and piece of turnip and cut them into quarters. Do not peel the onions, but wash them well. Arrange some of the vegetables in the bottom of the saucepan, place the lamb on top, then add the rest of the vegetables, the thyme and the peppercorns. Cover with cold water and bring it fairly quickly to the boil. Add 3 teaspoons salt and lower the heat at once, so that the liquid just trembles. Cook like this for 30 minutes per pound, plus 30 minutes. Skim off any scum that rises to the surface. At the end of the cooking time, remove the pan from the heat and leave the lamb 'resting' in the broth for 10 minutes or so. 'Punch-nep' (*see* page 144) is delicious with boiled lamb, and you can serve one of the following sauces:

Laver Sauce

Laver is a seaweed found on rock and sand coasts up and down western Britain, although it has always been a peculiarly Welsh delicacy. It clings to the rocks at low tide like wet silk, brownish-green in colour, and shaped like lettuce leaves. If you are gathering it yourself, collect as much as you can as, once prepared, it freezes well. Wash the laver thoroughly, to get rid of sand and small shells.

Put about 2 inches of water in a pan and add plenty of salt. Simmer the laver in this until very tender – about 2½ hours. Drain it well, then pack it into polythene bags, label it clearly as it looks very like spinach, and freeze it. It will also keep well in a container with a well-fitting lid, in the fridge.

For the sauce, take about 8 oz of laver, chop it finely and reheat it in the juice of 2 Seville oranges (these also freeze well), or of 1 orange and 1 lemon. Season it with salt and pepper and serve it hot with the boiled lamb; its delicate iodine flavour blends perfectly with the meat.

Caper Sauce

Melt 1½ oz butter in a saucepan and stir in 1½ oz flour. Add, slowly, ¾ pint of broth taken from the pan in which the lamb is cooking. Stir until the sauce is thick and then let it simmer for 20 minutes. Stir in 1 tablespoon of thick cream, 2 teaspoons of caper vinegar and 3 tablespoons drained capers. Taste for seasoning and serve.

Onion Sauce

Cook this for the same length of time as the lamb.

3 large onions	¾ pint hot milk
2 oz butter	1 bayleaf
2 oz flour	Salt, pepper, nutmeg

Melt the butter in a saucepan and add the finely sliced onions. Let them cook gently, with a lid on the pan, for about 15 minutes, until they are soft and transparent. Stir in the flour, and, off the heat, the hot milk, adding it gradually until you have a smooth sauce. Put in the bayleaf and a little salt and simmer very gently, stirring occasionally, until the lamb is ready. Remove the bayleaf, add 3 tablespoons cream and check the seasoning, adding salt, freshly-ground black pepper and nutmeg to taste.

Cold Lamb and Rice Salad

12 oz Basmati rice
1 tblsp dressing, made with
lemon juice
1 small onion
1 clove garlic
2 teasps crushed coriander
2 teasps chopped fresh
marjoram

½ lb cold lamb, chopped
3 large tomatoes, skinned
and chopped
A handful or two of cold,
cooked, broad beans
Salt, pepper

Wash the rice, then boil it for 12 minutes. Drain it very thoroughly. While it is still warm, stir in the dressing, the finely chopped onion and garlic, marjoram and coriander. Add the lamb, tomatoes and broad beans when the rice is cold, mixing them in gently. This is a delicious salad for a summer buffet supper.

Lamb Baked with Vegetables

1 leg or loin of lamb –
about 2½-3 lb
6 cloves garlic
Fresh thyme, marjoram
and rosemary
1 lb new potatoes

2 tumblers white wine
1 lb courgettes
1 large aubergine
1 lb large tomatoes
Salt and pepper

Ask the butcher to chop the lamb through the bone in 4 or 5 places, but not right through the meat, so that it stays in one piece. Chop two of the garlic cloves and the herbs finely and rub this mixture into the meat. Heat the oven to 400° F, arrange the meat in a large roasting dish, pour a little olive oil over it and cook for 15 minutes, near the top of the oven. Meanwhile, scrape the potatoes, then add them to the meat with a tumbler of wine and the rest of the garlic. Lower the oven heat to 325° F. Cook for another 45 minutes, turning the potatoes once or twice. Cut the courgettes and aubergine into thick slices, sprinkle them with salt and leave them to drain, in a colander, for about 30 minutes. Peel and chop the tomatoes; add these three vegetables, and the rest of the wine, to the meat and potatoes, mixing everything together round the meat with a wooden spoon and fork. Return to the oven to cook for another 35 minutes, or until the lamb and potatoes are tender. It is impossible to over-cook this dish and it is a wonderful late-summer Sunday lunch.

Lamb and Mixed Bean Stew

2 lb scrag end neck, in
  neat pieces
4 oz chick peas
2 oz haricot beans
1 oz red kidney beans
4 large sliced onions

6 whole cloves garlic
Good dripping
Thyme, rosemary and
  bayleaves
½ pint white wine
Pepper

To finish

2 oz fresh breadcrumbs
1 clove garlic

2 tblsps parsley
Rind ½ lemon

This should be made the day before you need it, to remove the fat from the top. Prepare the beans and chick peas according to the method on pages 55-6. Put half of them in a deep stoneware pot. Fry the onions, garlic, and sliced meat in the dripping until brown. Put them into the pot, bury the herbs in the middle and cover them with the rest of the beans. Pour in the wine and add a generous amount of pepper – no salt. Pour in enough water to cover the beans, cover the pot with foil and its lid and cook extremely slowly for 4-5 hours at 300° F. When the beans are soft, stir in plenty of salt, then leave to cool overnight. Next day, skim off the fat and reheat the stew. Put the bread, parsley, garlic and lemon peel in the blender and blend until all are finely chopped. Sprinkle this on the top of the beans and return to the oven, without a lid, until the breadcrumbs are crisp. Serve very hot, with plain green salad. Do not be tempted to use better quality lamb as scrag end has the best flavour.

Grilled Breast of Lamb

This is a lengthy dish to prepare, but each operation is not time-consuming in itself, and the end products – crisp juicy pieces of lamb, full of flavour, and a pint of delicious stock – are worth the extra trouble.

2 lb breast of lamb in
   one piece
2 carrots
1 large onion
1 pint water
Bouquet garni

Salt and pepper
Beaten egg
Mustard – Dijon
Seasoned breadcrumbs
2 lemons

Peel and slice the carrots and onion and make a bed of them for the lamb in a roasting tin. Season the meat and put it flat on top of the vegetables. Add the herbs and water, cover the tin with foil and cook in a low (300° F) oven for about 2½ hours. Let the meat cool a little, then slide out the bones using a sharp knife. Wrap the meat in the foil and weight it until cold. Strain the juices into a basin. Next day, remove any surplus fat from the meat, then cut it into narrow diagonal strips. Beat the egg, stir in 1-2 teaspoons mustard and dip the strips of meat in it before rolling them in the breadcrumbs. Leave them to dry on a rack. Grill, turning the strips over once or twice, for about 20 minutes. Serve very hot, on hot plates, with a good sloppy potato purée and plenty of lemon quarters.

Spiced Lamb to Taste like Venison

A boned leg or shoulder makes a good joint for this dish. It is excellent cold.

3 lb boned lamb,
   in one piece, but untied
6 oz brown sugar
Pinch ground cloves
Pinch ginger

½ teasp nutmeg
¼ oz saltpetre
½ teasp black pepper
1½ oz salt

Mix the spices together and rub them well into the meat, working into every crevice. Put the meat into a large bowl, cover with a cloth and keep it for a week in a cool place (longer if the weather is cold). Rub it from time to time, and turn it in the juices. When you are ready to cook the lamb, wipe off the spices and tie it firmly into a neat shape. Cook *very* gently, as for the boiled lamb on page 89. Serve with rowan or redcurrant jelly. The red cabbage recipe on page 129 is another good accompaniment.

PORK

I was sad to hear recently that a new, even leaner, breed of pig is being introduced. Soon pork will be as dry as turkey or veal, needing to be dressed up with sauces, or larded with extra fat to make it moist. It is the amount of fat on pork that makes it the succulent meat it is. For those who find it indigestible, try putting the joint into brine for 12 hours (*see* page 10) before cooking it by the French method.

English Roast Pork with Spiced Apples

A loin of pork produces better crackling than a leg, as there is a thicker layer of fat underneath the skin. Score the skin deeply so that the fat bastes the flesh underneath as it cooks. Rub the skin with salt and a little olive oil, and stand the joint on a rack over the roasting tin, so that the skin on the underside stays crisp as well. Roast for 30 minutes per pound at 375° F, plus 30 minutes, allowing 40-45 minutes over if the joint weighs less than 3 lb.

Spiced Apples

8 small Cox's Orange Pippins   Ground mixed spice
  (4 if they are large)   Dry cider
Butter

Peel the apples, but leave them whole. Melt a little butter in a saucepan and roll the apples in this, then dust each with a little of the spice. Put the apples into the roasting tin, underneath the pork, about an hour before the end of cooking time. When the pork is done, remove it to a warm dish, surround it with the apples, and make a gravy by skimming off most of the fat from the juices in the tin, adding a large glass of dry cider and while it is boiling, stirring in all the residual bits and pieces. Check the seasoning before pouring it into a gravy boat.

French Roast Pork with Herbs

Crackling is an English delicacy; in France, joints for roasting are sold without the skin.

2½ lb loin of pork, skin and bones removed
2 cloves garlic
Salt and pepper

3-4 tblsps chopped fresh herbs – a mixture of whatever is available
2 glasses white wine

Put the meat into brine for about 12 hours if you prefer, particularly if you intend to eat it cold. Cut the garlic into slivers, and distribute them over the inside of the meat; season with salt and freshly ground black pepper, then roll it up and tie it firmly with string. Mix a little salt with the chopped herbs, and sprinkle the fat of the pork with this mixture, pressing it well down all over. Cook the meat in a medium oven (350° F) for 35 minutes per pound, plus 45 minutes. A 2½ lb piece will take about 2 hours. Baste the joint frequently with the pan juices and white wine.

Galantine of Pork

A hand of pork is traditional for this, but I find a piece of boned shoulder does very well for a smaller quantity.

2½ lb shoulder pork
Pork bones and skin
2 pigs' trotters, split
2 large onions
Sprig of herbs –
    thyme, parsley, rosemary,
    celery, lemon peel

2 teasps salt
½ pint dry cider
6 black peppercorns
6 juniper berries
2 cloves garlic
1 tblsp chopped parsley

Put all the ingredients except the garlic and chopped parsley into a large pan and cover with cold water. Bring slowly to the boil, skim off any rising scum and simmer very gently for about 1½-2 hours, or until the meat is tender. Remove the meat and continue cooking the stock for another ½ hour, as you will be using it to make the jelly. Chop the meat roughly and mix it with the finely chopped garlic and parsley. Put it into an oblong terrine, and cover to keep it warm. Pour in just enough of the stock (check seasoning) to cover the meat; strain the rest of the stock into a large bowl; leave the pork and the stock in a cool place to set overnight. Next day, turn out the galantine (stand the terrine in a bowl of very hot water for 3 or 4 minutes to loosen it) and put it on a long dish. Surround it with the roughly chopped jelly.

Pork and Beans

A version of *cassoulet* which is cheaper and easier but just as filling.

2 lb belly pork	6 cloves garlic
4 portions of preserved chicken (*see* page 13)	Salt and pepper
	1 15 oz can Italian tomatoes
1 lb pure pork sausages, smoked if possible	Large bunch thyme and rosemary
10 oz haricot beans	A little red wine
4 onions	

Prepare the beans by bring them to the boil and leaving them to soak for 45 minutes (*see* page 173). Cut the pork into large chunks and the onions into quarters; peel the garlic. Put the pork into a frying-pan and cook it gently until the fat starts to run. Raise the heat and fry it and the onions and garlic until brown. Season with plenty of freshly-ground pepper, and a little salt. Put half the drained beans into a stoneware pot with a lid, arrange the pork and onions on top, then cover with the rest of the beans. Empty the tin of tomatoes in, add the herbs, and cover the contents with a mixture of water and red wine. Cover with butter paper, foil and the lid and cook in a low oven for 2½ hours. Check occasionally to see that the beans aren't absorbing too much liquid. Smoke the sausages in the fish-smoker if you have one, or fry them until brown all over; add them to the pot and return it to the oven for another 45 minutes. Half-an-hour before you are ready to eat, add the pieces of preserved chicken, if you are using it (you can use fresh chicken by browning it and adding it with the sausages). Check the seasoning before serving, as it will probably need more salt. This dish is extremely good-tempered and will keep hot, or stand reheating any number of times.

Salt Pork

3 lb belly pork, which has been in the brine jar for at least a week (*see* page 10)	2 leeks
	Bunch of herbs
	6 peppercorns
2 carrots	6 juniper berries
2 onions	1 Savoy cabbage

Tie the meat into a neat roll and put it into a large pan; cover it with cold water and bring it to the boil. Taste the water, and if it is too salty, throw it away and start with a fresh lot. Add all the vegetables and seasonings except the cabbage. Simmer gently for 30 minutes per pound. Half an hour before the pork is ready, quarter the cabbage and add it to the pan. Serve the meat surrounded by the cabbage, and with green lentils, or potatoes boiled in their skins. Have several different mustards on the table, and a jar of pickled damsons (page 170), or walnuts. The fat of salt pork is very good, especially cold.

Home-made Sausages

You should be able to buy sausage skins from any butcher who makes his own sausages (they may need soaking in cold water first, if they have been stored in salt, and are hard). A sausage-making attachment is available to fit the mincer of the Kenwood Chef, but if all this sounds too complicated, simply make up the sausage-meat, shape it into flat cakes and dip it in lightly-beaten egg-white before frying.

2 lb belly pork, skin and bones removed	Salt, pepper
¼ lb back pork fat	2 oz white breadcrumbs
1 clove garlic	2 tblsps white wine
2-3 tblsps finely chopped parsley, thyme and celery leaves	2 oz pistachio nuts (optional)

Put the pork, fat and garlic through the fine screen on the mincer. Mix in thoroughly the herbs, seasonings, breadcrumbs and wine, and the chopped pistachio nuts if you are using them. Either shape this mixture into small flat cakes, or put it through the mincer again, this time with the sausage filler and skins attached. Make each sausage about 4″ long before twisting the skin to form the next link. They can then be used as ordinary sausages, and are very suitable for the following recipe which is a glamorous version of toad-in-the-hole.

Saucisses en Brioche

¼ oz dried yeast	mix these together and leave
Pinch sugar	for 10-15 minutes until the
2 tblsps warm milk	yeast froths

8 oz plain flour	1 lb sausages (see above, or any
Pinch salt	kind which has a minimal
2 eggs	proportion of cereal to pork)
4 oz soft butter	

Sift the flour and salt into a bowl and leave it in a warm place while waiting for the yeast to dissolve. Make a well in the middle of the flour, break in the eggs, then add the frothy yeast and milk. Beat the flour into the eggs until you have a smooth dough, then work in the butter, cut into small pieces. The dough will be sticky and slippery, but persevere, adding sprinkles of flour when necessary, until you have a springy ball of dough which leaves the bowl clean. Cut a deep cross into it, cover with a cloth, and leave in a warm place for about 2 hours, or until it has doubled in size. Knead it again, cover, and leave it in a cool place until you are ready to use it. About 2 hours before you want to eat, cover the sausages with cold water in a saucepan and bring them slowly to simmering point. Simmer for about 30 minutes. Drain them and skin them as soon as they are cool enough to handle. Flatten out the dough on a greased baking sheet, into a rectangle and arrange the warm sausages down the centre. Wrap the dough round the sausages and pinch all the edges firmly together; smooth the parcel with a wet palette knife, and brush with top-of-the-milk. Leave to prove while you heat the oven to 375° F. Bake the brioche for about 30 minutes, or until golden brown. Serve it as a main dish, perhaps with the dish of cabbage with mustard cream on page 128.

'A Leg of Pork to Taste Like Wild Boar'

Having tasted wild boar in Belgium, I can vouch for the success of this recipe. As it is equally good cold, it is a useful Christmas dish, helping to enliven the slices of cold turkey. As a leg of pork is rather large, half a leg, or a piece of rolled loin or shoulder are all good substitutes.

3 lb boned and skinned pork

Marinade

½ pint red wine
¼ pint red wine vinegar
Salt
1 sliced carrot

2 sliced onions
Bayleaves, thyme, juniper berries, cloves, peppercorns

Put all the marinade ingredients into a saucepan and boil them for 5 minutes. Let the marinade get quite cold; score the pork fat with a sharp knife, put it in a bowl and pour the cold marinade over it. Cover it and leave it in a cool place for 5-6 days, turning it once or twice a day. Tie the meat into a neat shape, and brown it well all over in a little olive oil. Heat the marinade and strain it through a sieve over the meat. Cover the pan and either braise it on top of the stove for about 30 minutes to the pound, or in a low oven (275° F) for about 2½ hours. When the meat is tender, remove it from the pan. Skim off some of the fat from the juices. Blend a teaspoon of cornflour with a little cold water and stir it into the pan juices. Cook for a minute or two and then add 2-3 tablespoons of redcurrant jelly (or better still, rowan jelly), stirring until it dissolves. Taste for seasoning; it will probably need salt, and you can add a little port if you have any. Chestnut purée goes well with this; so does red cabbage, but best of all is a dish of potatoes cooked with juniper berries (page 141) which comes from the Ardennes, where wild boar is to be found on many good restaurant menus.

Bollito Misto

This mixture of boiled meat is an Italian one, but the meat has to be more tactfully chosen for English stomachs.

1½ lb silverside of beef
1 rasher streaky bacon
3-4 pigs' trotters, split
2-3 salted calves' tongues
2 lb salt pork

1 small boiling fowl
Flavouring vegetables and
    herbs
Peppercorns
Salt

Lard the beef with the rasher of bacon cut into strips, and put it, with the trotters, tongues and salt pork into a very large saucepan. Cover with cold water and bring slowly to the boil. Add the veg-etables – carrots, onions, a parsnip, a stick of celery; and the herbs – thyme, parsley, 2 bayleaves, as well as 10 peppercorns and a table-spoon of salt. Simmer gently for 1 hour. Add the chicken and sausage (a French or Italian garlic sausage is best) and simmer gently for another 1½ hours. All the meat should be very tender and almost falling off the bones. In another saucepan cook some floury potatoes in their skins, and a few carrots. Have a large meat dish warming in the oven. Pile the various meats in the middle and sur-round with the potatoes and carrots. Have ready a large bowl of *salsa verde* (*see* page 64). This is not an elegant, or cheap dish, but it is generous, and perfect for a cold day.

Poultry &
Some Game

Poultry and Some Game

It is worth paying a little more for a fresh, rather than frozen chicken, and trying to buy a free-range bird if you can. Use supermarket chickens for casseroles, improving the flavour with herbs, tomatoes, garlic and wine. Hare and venison are the cheapest game, especially if you are willing to skin the hare yourself. Remember to check on exactly how long game has been hung before you buy it.

English Roast Chicken

1 3½ lb fresh chicken, its giblets and liver
4 oz streaky bacon rashers, home-cured
1 lb pork chipolatas

Stuffing

The chicken liver, finely chopped
1 oz butter
1 small onion
3 oz fresh breadcrumbs

1 tblsp chopped fresh herbs
1 teasp grated lemon rind
Salt and pepper
A little beaten egg

Melt the butter and cook the chopped chicken liver in it. Slice the onion finely and add it to the liver; continue to cook gently until the onion is soft. Stir in the breadcrumbs, herbs, lemon rind, salt and freshly-ground pepper; mix thoroughly and bind with beaten egg. Put the chicken giblets in a pan with just enough water to cover them, a little salt and pepper, and a bunch of flavouring herbs. Bring very slowly to simmering point, and simmer while the chicken cooks. Heat the oven to 400° F. Stuff the chicken and close the cavity with a skewer. Season it with pepper and a little salt and lay it on its side, covering it with two bacon rashers. Roast for 30 minutes. Turn it on to its other side and cover with two more rashers. Keeping the sausages linked together, add them to the roasting tin with the chicken, together with a little extra dripping if necessary. Return to the oven for another 30 minutes. Now put the chicken on its back, with another rasher over its breast, basting it well with the pan juices. Turn the sausages over. Replace the tin in the oven and continue roasting for a final 30 minutes. Cooking the bird first on one side, then on the other, means that the legs cook at the same time as the breast. Dish the chicken on to a warm meat plate, arranging the bacon around it and the sausages in a garland over its breast; remove the skewer. Put it in the switched-off oven, with the door ajar, while you make the gravy. Drain off most of the fat from the roasting tin and add the giblet stock. Bring to the boil, stirring in all the bits and pieces sticking to the pan. Mix 1 teaspoon corn-flour with a little water and add it to the gravy; stir until thickened and boiling, check the seasoning and pour into a sauce-boat. English roast chicken is incomplete without bread sauce:

¾ pint milk	3 thick slices bread without crusts
1 sliced onion	Salt, pepper and nutmeg
2 cloves	2 tblsps double cream

Infuse the onion and cloves in the milk over a low heat for 15 min-utes. Remove the cloves, add the bread, cut into rough cubes, a little salt, pepper and nutmeg, and simmer gently until the onion is soft. Put the sauce into the blender – if it looks too thick, add a little of the giblet stock. Return it to the pan, add the cream, then check the seasoning.

English roast chicken is good in winter. In summer the French method is more suitable.

French Roast Chicken

1 3½ lb chicken, fresh, and free-range if possible	2 cloves garlic
4 oz butter	Chopped fresh tarragon
	Salt and pepper

Take half the butter and mix it with the chopped tarragon and garlic, together with a little salt, and plenty of pepper. Put it into the bird's cavity. Make a giblet stock as above, and heat the oven to 400° F. Again, put the bird on its side in the roasting tin, this time spreading some of the butter over it. Roast for 30 minutes, turn it on to its other side, spread it with more butter and roast for another 30 minutes. Finally, turn the bird on its back and baste the breast with the pan juices; return it to the oven and baste frequently during the final 30 minutes. Make the gravy as above, but without draining off the butter, or thickening it. A little white wine is a good addition.

Chicken and Orange Pilau from Afghanistan

1 large chicken – a frozen one will do

Rind of 4 oranges
Juice of 2 oranges
2 sliced oranges
4 oz sultanas
3 oz almonds

3 oz hazelnuts
1 oz butter
Triple strength orange flower
    water (from chemists)
4 tblsps clear honey

1 lb onions
2 cloves garlic

Good dripping
½ pint stock

12 oz Basmati rice
1 packet saffron threads

Salt

First stage: soak the orange rind (removed with a potato peeler) in water for an hour, changing the water once. Soak the sultanas in a separate bowl, or they will absorb the bitterness of the peel. Slice 2 of the peeled oranges. Drain the orange peel, chop it and the nuts, and cook them both in the butter, adding the drained sultanas and the orange slices. Add the juice of the two remaining peeled oranges, 2 tablespoons orange flower water, and the honey. Cook gently together for about 15 minutes, then drain the fruit and nuts and reserve the syrup.

Second stage: chop the onions and garlic and melt them in the dripping. Cut the chicken into portions, removing the skin, brown it with the onions, pour on the stock and cook until the chicken is tender – about 45 minutes. Drain and reserve the stock (taste it for seasoning).

Third stage: wash the rice under the cold tap until the water runs clear. Put 2 pints water in a saucepan with 2 teaspoons salt and bring it to the boil. Put the saffron threads into a cup and cover with a very little hot water – leave to infuse for 15 minutes, then add this strained infusion to the water in which you are cooking the rice. Cook the rice for 11-12 minutes – it should still have a bite to it. Drain thoroughly.

Fourth stage: arrange a layer of rice in the bottom of a large oven-proof dish, cover with the chicken pieces and onion, then sprinkle the fruit and nut mixture over the chicken. Spread the rest of the rice over the top, moisten it with the reserved chicken stock, then trickle the orange and honey syrup over the top. Cover the dish with butter papers and heat at 350° F for 45 minutes. Lower the heat to 225° F until you are ready to eat.

Although fairly lengthy to make, this is an excellent and unusual party dish which can be made long in advance, reheated, and kept hot almost indefinitely.

Poulet Richel

One of the few chicken dishes with which you can drink a powerful claret.

4 oz shin beef	1 sliced carrot
1 tblsp beef dripping	1 bayleaf
1 large onion	1 tblsp tomato purée

Melt the beef dripping and brown the sliced beef in it, then the sliced onion and carrot. Add the bayleaf and tomato purée and a pinch of salt. Cover, barely, with cold water, bring slowly to the boil, then simmer gently for 2 hours (this can be done in a low oven). Strain the stock and reduce it to ½ pint. Reserve.

1 large free-range chicken　　2 sprigs thyme
4 oz belly pork　　　　　　½ pint thick cream
1 large onion　　　　　　　¼ pint claret (dregs from
Salt　　　　　　　　　　　　　　a decanted bottle)
1 dstsp green peppercorns

Chop the pork into small cubes and heat it in a heavy casserole until the fat runs. Chop the onion finely and add it to the pork, cooking gently until the onion is transparent. Season the chicken with salt and seal it all over with the pork and onion, letting the onion brown and caramelize, but being careful not to let it burn; the flavour of the browned onion is important in the finished sauce. Add the crushed peppercorns, the thyme, the hot stock and the wine and bubble fiercely for a minute or two. Put on the lid and transfer the pan to a moderate (350° F) oven for an hour, basting frequently. When the chicken is tender, transfer it to a warm dish. Reduce the pan juices by about one-third, then pour in the cream, stirring well. Boil fast until the sauce thickens, then taste for seasoning. Do not strain out the bits and pieces of pork, onion, etc. Carve the chicken and pour the sauce over it.

Fried Chicken

A supermarket chicken, defrosted, jointed and dipped in seasoned flour, egg and breadcrumbs, fried in hot olive oil for 25 minutes and carefully drained, is very good with the tarator sauce on page 69, especially if it has marinated in garlic and lemon juice for an hour or two before being egg-and-breadcrumbed. Cold fried chicken is delicious for picnics.

CAPON

A more sympathetic bird for a small family at Christmas than a thumping great turkey, capon also has more flavour. You can cook it in any of the ways given for chicken. Here is a recipe for a Christmas stuffiing:

Pork, Orange and Walnut Stuffing

This quantity is enough for a 6 lb capon.

2 large Cox's apples
1 clove garlic
Liver of the bird

1 small onion
8 oz belly pork

Put all the above ingredients through the medium screen of the mincer, then cook gently for 15-20 minutes in a small amount of butter.

1 tblsp clear honey
Grated rind and juice of
   2 oranges
3 oz fresh breadcrumbs

Salt, freshly ground pepper
1 tblsp chopped parsley
2 oz walnuts, chopped
1 dstsp coriander

Add the above ingredients to the mixture in the pan, and bind with one beaten egg. Keep this in a cool place overnight to give the flavours a chance to blend. Stuff the capon with it, and roast it for 25 minutes per pound at 375° F plus 25 minutes, basting frequently with butter and white wine. Turn the oven down a little at half-time if the bird is cooking too fast.

TURKEY

One of the best ways of dealing with this often rather dry and boring bird is the Victorian recipe for boiling it and serving it with a celery sauce. A small 6-8 lb turkey is obviously as large as is practical, unless you have a ham kettle in which to cook it.

Boiled Turkey with Celery Sauce, Veal Stuffing

1 6-8 lb turkey

For the stuffing:

8 oz lean veal
6 oz fat bacon
2 oz fresh breadcrumbs
Large pinch grated nutmeg

Pinch ground cloves
1 large egg
Salt and pepper

Mince the veal and bacon, mix them well with all the other ingredients and stuff the turkey with this, sewing up all the openings with a needle and thread. Don't stuff it too tightly as the breadcrumbs will swell.

For the broth:

2 split pigs' trotters	Sprig of mixed herbs
2 large carrots	10 black peppercorns
2 large onions, each stuck	1 tblsp salt
with a clove	Glass of white wine

Put all these ingredients into the largest saucepan you have and add 4 pints of water. Bring to the boil and simmer for 15 minutes before adding the turkey – breast down. Bring carefully back to the boil, adding more water if necessary to cover the bird. Simmer gently for 1¾ hours, or until a leg will part easily from the body of the turkey.

For the sauce:

1 head of celery	1 oz each of butter and flour
(or the outside stalks of	Salt, freshly ground pepper
2 heads)	and nutmeg
A béchamel sauce	¼ pint double cream
made with ½ pint milk,	

Wash the celery carefully, cut it into strips and poach it until tender in a little broth taken from the cooking turkey. Drain it and put it through the vegetable-mill straight into the waiting béchamel (which should have been cooking for at least 15 minutes beforehand). Stir very well and add the cream; heat until nearly boiling, check the seasoning, adding nutmeg as well as salt and pepper, and serve with the turkey.

GOOSE

Now very expensive, but still the best Christmas dish of all.

Roast Goose with Buckwheat, and Fruit Stuffing

1 large goose
¾ pint dry cider for basting

Stuffing :

Goose liver
1 oz butter
1 small onion
½ lb dried apricots,
   soaked overnight and
   drained
1 lb peeled and cored
   Cox's apples

4 tblsps fresh breadcrumbs
Rind and juice of
   1 sweet orange
Juice of 1 Seville orange
Salt and pepper

Blanch the liver for 10-15 minutes in boiling salted water. Melt the finely chopped onion in the butter, add the chopped liver, apricots and apples. Cook for 5 minutes, then add the breadcrumbs, orange rind and juices, salt, and freshly ground pepper. Stir well, remove from the heat and leave to cool. Stuff the goose with this and sew up the cavity. Season the goose with salt and pepper and lie it on its side on a grid in the roasting tin. Roast it for 20 minutes per pound, plus 35 minutes at 375° F, turning it over on to its other side after 30 minutes, then on to its back after another 30 minutes. Baste it with the cider. Lower the heat to 350° F if it is cooking too fast.

Make 1 pint of stock from the goose giblets, some herbs, an onion and the usual seasonings. Melt a little dripping in a heavy casserole and stir 10 oz buckwheat around it in until each grain is coated. Pour on the hot, strained, stock, add 1 teaspon salt and cook fast until almost all the stock is absorbed. Cover the pan tightly, lower the heat and cook very gently until the buckwheat is just tender.

Use the pan juices, skimmed of their copious fat, and more cider to make gravy for the goose.

DUCK

Almost as extravagant as goose, as there is so little meat in proportion to bone, but equally delicious.

Roast Duck with Dumplings and Blackcurrant Sauce

Roast the duck on a rack over the roasting tin, cooking it first on one side, then on the other, and finally on its back, to ensure that the legs are cooked at the same time as the rest of it. 1½ hours at 375° F should be enough for a 3 lb duck – the leg will part easily from the body when it is cooked.

CZECH DUMPLINGS

4 oz fresh breadcrumbs
4 oz plain flour
2 teasps baking powder
Pinch mixed spice

3 oz suet
1 teasp salt
Freshly ground pepper

Mix all the dry ingredients, then add enough cold water to make a firm dough. Shape the mixture into a long roll which will fit one of your saucepans. Flour a piece of foil and fold the dumpling into it, making sure that the edges are tightly folded together, but leaving room for the dumpling to swell. Cook it in boiling water for one hour.

If there are no fresh or frozen blackcurrants available, you can use a jar of good-quality blackcurrant jam, sharpened with a little lemon juice, or it will be too sweet. Or, cook 1 lb blackcurrants with a little brown sugar, and very little water until they are soft. Season with a little mixed spice and serve as it is, only putting the sauce through the vegetable-mill if you strongly object to the pips.

Serve the dumpling cut in slices with the duck and sauce; any vegetables should be served separately.

Spiced Duck

1 3-4 lb duck	2 crushed peppercorns
6 oz block salt	1 teasp mixed spice
1 crumbled bayleaf	

Mix the salt with the spices and bayleaf and rub this mixture all over the duck, inside and out. Leave it in a deep bowl in a cool place for 3 days, rubbing it twice daily with the brine. Take it out and wipe it; put it into a casserole and cover it with water. Cook it, without a lid (so that the skin of the breast will turn pale gold and crispen a little, as it floats in the water) for 2 hours at 325° F. Let it get quite cold; then serve it with an orange and watercress salad.

GAME

Rowan Jelly

This is so good with game that it is worth making an expedition, after the first September frosts, to gather rowan berries. The rowan, or mountain ash, grows wild all over the country, and in many suburban gardens as well. It is easily distinguishable by its clusters of bright orange-red berries.

1 large panful of berries, the largest stalks and leaves removed	1 lb sugar for each pint of juice
Water to cover	

Cover the berries with water, bring them slowly to the boil, and simmer until soft, squashing the fruit with a wooden spoon now and them. Tip the contents of the pan into a jelly bag or old pillowcase and allow it to drip overnight into a large bowl. Next day, measure the juice, and add a pound of sugar for each pint. Heat gently, stirring occasionally, until the sugar has dissolved, then boil fast until the setting point is reached. (Test by dropping a little on a saucer; if a skin forms on the surface of the drop, it is ready.) Pot in warm jars and label. This jelly never sets very firmly; a useful quality when adding it to sauces as it melts very quickly. If you prefer a firmer set, add a few windfall apples to the berries as they cook. Rowan jelly keeps very well, and is better a year after making, although, of course, it can be used immediately. Its bitterness complements the sweet, strong flavour of game.

Roast Venison

3 lb haunch of venison,
  well-hung
6 oz home-cured bacon for
  larding

1 roasting bag
2 tblsps good dripping
Salt, pepper

Marinade

½ pint red wine
4 tblsps olive oil
6 black peppercorns
6 crushed juniper berries

¼ pint red wine vinegar
Thyme, bayleaves, orange
  and lemon peel
2 teasps salt

Mix all the marinade ingredients together in a large bowl, and leaves the venison in it for 24 hours, turning now and then. When you are ready to cook it, take it out of the marinade and wipe it; cut the bacon into strips, and using a larding needle, push them into the meat, distributing them evenly. Heat the oven to 350° F; salt and pepper the venison, smear it with the dripping, and put it into the roasting bag (the modern equivalent of the huff-paste in which venison was once wrapped before roasting; it prevents the meat from drying out in the same way as the huff-paste did, but lets it brown at the same time). Fasten the neck of the bag loosely, put the whole thing into a roasting tin and cook it for 20 minutes per pound, plus 20 minutes.

Sweet Sauce for Venison

'Currant Jelly warmed, which is much the best; or two or three Glasses of red Wine, sweetened with Sugar, and simmered a few Minutes on the Fire'. Richard Bradley, *The Country Housewife*, 1753.

You can substitute rowan for currant jelly, and either use port as a sauce, or add a few cloves and a little nutmeg to Richard Bradley's recipe.

Venison Casserole with Prunes

2 lb stewing venison	8 oz salt pork
Marinade as for roast venison	2 large onions
12 oz best prunes	Salt and pepper
½ pint red wine	Small glass port

Cut the venison into cubes and marinate it overnight. Soak the prunes in the red wine overnight also. Next day, cut the salt pork into strips and heat them until the fat runs. Brown the drained venison in this, then add the sliced onions. Add the prunes and their wine, and the strained marinade. Bury the herbs from the marinade amongst the meat. Put it all into an ovenproof pot with 2 teaspoons of salt and a generous amount of freshly-ground pepper. Cover the pot with a layer of butter paper, a layer of foil, then the lid, and cook in a low (300° F) oven for 3 hours, or until the meat is very tender. Stir in the port, check the seasoning, then serve it with potato and celeriac purée.

HARE

It should be hung, by the back legs, for a week to 10 days, depending on the weather; check with the butcher.

Lepre in Agrodolce

(Hare in a sweet and sour sauce.) A very good recipe in which the chocolate loses its identity but gives great richness to the sauce.

1 hare, jointed	¼ pint red wine vinegar
Marinade as for roast venison	2 oz sultanas
4 oz streaky bacon	2 oz good cooking chocolate
1 tblsp flour	2 oz pine nuts (or almonds)
1 oz brown sugar	

Marinate the hare overnight, then drain it and strain the marinade into a saucepan (keep the herbs). Brown the pieces of hare with the fat bacon cut into cubes; sprinkle with the flour and mix well. Heat the marinade and pour it over the top, bury the herbs amongst the pieces of hare, stir in salt and pepper, cover the casserole and cook very gently for 1½ hours. Dissolve the sugar in the vinegar, then add the sultanas and simmer for 15 minutes. Grate the chocolate and add it to the vinegar and sugar. Stir until smooth, then pour it into the casserole, together with the pine nuts or almonds. Cook for another 1½ hours, until the meat is almost falling off the bones. Cool, and reheat the next day. Serve it with a mound of buttery *tagliatelle*.

Cumbrian Hare with Rowan Jelly

You *can* use redcurrant jelly, in which case add the juice of a lemon, or better still, a Seville orange.

Front and back legs of a large hare	Large sprig of thyme
3 small onions, each stuck with 2 cloves	1 lb jar rowan jelly
	1 wineglass port
	Salt and pepper

Brown the pieces of hare well in good dripping. Pack them into a stoneware pot. Brown the whole, peeled onions in the same dripping and add them to the hare. Bury the thyme amongst the meat and onions and empty the pot of jelly over it all. Add some salt, plenty of pepper, and the port. Cover with a double layer of foil and the lid, stand the casserole in a baking-tin of hot water and cook very slowly (250° F) for at least 3 hours. Braised celery goes well with this dish.

Saddle of Hare with Cream

An alarming dish to make for the first time, as the cream curdles. However, it turns out all right in the end.

1 saddle of hare, marinated overnight in the marinade on page 112	2 rashers streaky bacon
	6 oz double cream
Salt and pepper	1 teasp cornflour

Remove the hare from the marinade, season it, and wrap it in the bacon. Put it into a fireproof dish which just holds it. Heat the marinade and pour it, bubbling, over the hare. Put the dish, uncovered, into a hot (400° F) oven and cook for 20 minutes. Pour the cream in, cover the dish and cook for a further 15 minutes. The meat should be slightly underdone. Put the saddle on a warm dish and pour the curdled cooking juices into a small saucepan. Add the cornflour, mixed with a little cold water, and bring to the boil, stirring hard. The sauce will become smooth and coffee-coloured; check the seasoning and serve with cooked, finely chopped beetroot, heated in a little butter and sprinkled with caraway seeds.

PHEASANT

Roast Pheasant with Red Cabbage

1 large red cabbage, prepared according to the recipe on page 129; it should be made well in advance, preferably the day before.

1 large red cabbage	4 rashers streaky bacon
1 brace pheasants, well-hung (at least ten days), plucked and drawn.	Salt and pepper Crushed juniper berries

Season the birds, inside and out, with salt, pepper and the crushed juniper berries. Spread the bacon rashers over the bottom of a roasting tin and put the birds on top, breast down. Roast them for 40 minutes at 425° F, before turning them breast up and cooking for another 10 minutes. Pile the red cabbage on a large serving dish and arrange the pheasants and their bacon on top.

Pheasant Casserole with Forcemeat Balls

1 large old cock pheasant	Large bunch thyme
Dripping	½ bottle red wine
2 onions, quartered	Salt and pepper
12 cloves garlic	

Forcemeat balls:

4 oz fresh breadcrumbs	Pinch dried thyme
2 oz suet	Scrap lemon rind
1 clove garlic	Salt and pepper
2 oz bacon	Beaten egg
1 tblsp parsley	Dripping

Brown the pheasant in a little dripping with the quartered onions and the peeled garlic cloves. Pack into a stoneware pot and bury the thyme in the middle. Sprinkle 1 tablespoon flour into the fat in the pan and then blend in the wine. Season with salt and freshly ground pepper, bring to the boil and pour over the pheasant. Cover tightly and cook gently in the oven (about 325° F) for 2-3 hours, or until the meat is tender. Mix the forcemeat ingredients together, chopping the garlic, parsley, bacon and lemon rind finely, and bind with the egg. Make little flattened balls the size of walnuts and fry in dripping until crisp and brown; drain them well on kitchen paper and serve them in a separate dish.

SNIPE

Delicious litle birds, distinctive by their long beaks.

Snipe with Vine Leaves

4 snipe, plucked but undrawn	Chopped marjoram
1 dozen large vine leaves	2 teasps brandy
4 large pieces fried bread	Salt and pepper
3 oz butter	

Blanch the vine leaves for 5 minutes in boiling salted water, then drain them carefully. Season the snipe, smear each with butter, then wrap them in the vineleaves. Fit them into a casserole, cover with a butter paper, then the lid. Cook at 425° F for 25 minutes. Have ready the pieces of bread, fried in a mixture of butter and oil, on a large dish. Scoop the entrails out of the snipe into a small pan, stir in the brandy, marjoram and salt and pepper, and when very hot, spread a little on each piece of bread. Sit a snipe, still in its vine leaves, on top of each and serve piping hot.

Wild Duck with Blackberries

2 wild duck, plucked & drawn	Salt and pepper
Their livers	2 oz butter
½ lb fresh blackberries (preferably wild)	2 bacon rashers

Heat the oven to 400° F. Stuff each duck with its liver, 4 oz blackberries, 1 oz butter and a little seasoning. Arrange the bacon rashers over them and roast for 35 minutes (longer if they are large). You can serve more blackberries, cooked with a very little brown sugar and a small glass of port, as a sauce.

PIGEONS

Pigeons used to be extremely cheap, but no longer, unless you can shoot them yourself. They are still worth cooking, by any long, slow method, as they are often tough.

Italian Casseroled Pigeons with Anchovies

4 fat pigeons	Grated rind 1 orange
1 tin anchovy fillets, drained	2-3 tblsps olive oil
2 cloves garlic	6 tblsps wine vinegar
Bunch of parsley	Salt and pepper
Grated rind 1 lemon	

Chop the garlic, parsley and anchovies and mix with the orange and lemon peel. Stuff the pigeons' cavities with a little of this mixture, then brown each pigeon all over in the olive oil. Put in a casserole with the rest of the anchovy mixture, the wine vinegar, and enough water to come halfway up the birds. Bring to the boil, add a little salt and plenty of black pepper, cover the pan tightly, lower the heat and cook extremely gently for 2½ hours, until the meat begins to drop from the bones. Remove the pigeons to a dish, reduce the liquid in the pan by about a third, and thicken it with 1 tblsp butter worked with 1 tblsp flour, added a small piece at a time to the boiling gravy. Pour this sauce over the pigeons and serve.

A Bisk of Pigeons

'Wash and parboil your Pigeons, put them into strong Broth, and stew them; make for them a Ragou with Gravy, Artichoke-bottoms, and Onions; season them with savoury Seasonings, the Juice of Lemons, and Lemons diced, Bacon cut as for Lard, Mushrooms, Truffles, and Morilles; pour the broth into a Dish with carved and dried Sippets; then place the Pigeons, and pour on the Ragou. Garnish with scalded Parsley, Beet-root, and Lemons.' Richard Bradley. *The Country Housewife*, 1753.

Vegetables

Vegetables

Despite the rising popularity of vegetarian diets and the present interest in growing vegetables in whatever patch of earth is available, we still mistreat them. In autumn 1977, brussels sprouts were 8p a pound, but there were plenty of people who were prepared to pay twice that for frozen ones, which would be tasteless and mushy once cooked. Elaborate vegetable dishes can be meals in themselves, and just a little butter and chopped parsley can transport winter carrots to realms of glory.

GLOBE ARTICHOKES

If you are buying them, the simplest way of cooking them is probably the best: in plenty of boiling salted water for 35 minutes, or until a leaf from the base comes away easily, then drained and served with lots of melted butter. If you grow your own (*see* page 22), you can afford to be more adventurous.

Greek Stuffed Artichokes

4 large artichokes	1 lb shelled broad beans
Lemon juice	Parsley and marjoram
2 cloves garlic	Salt and pepper
2 chopped onions	3 tblsps olive oil

Trim the stalks and cut off about an inch from the tops. You should be able to see the whiskery choke; remove it carefully with a sharp knife and rub the hollow with lemon juice. Fill each cavity with chopped onion and garlic, the chopped herbs and a little salt and pepper. Put the broad beans into a heavy casserole and arrange the artichokes on top. Pour in the olive oil and a tablespoon of lemon juice. Cover with cold water, add a little salt and cover the pan. Simmer slowly, either in a low oven or on top of the stove, until a leaf parts easily from the artichokes. Remove the lid, raise the heat and boil fast to evaporate the water. When the oil begins to spit, take them off the heat and allow to get quite cold. Serve them with an extra squeeze of lemon juice.

JERUSALEM ARTICHOKES

These look more like potatoes than anything else, and are, if anything, easier to grow. They need considerable space as they are tall-growing. One of the explanations of their name is that it comes from the Italian word for sunflower, *girasole*, because the leaves of both are so similar. They are fiddly to peel, so parboil them in their skins and finish cooking them in one of the following ways:

Artichokes in Red Wine

Slice the peeled and partly cooked artichokes thickly and put them in a pan with a large glass of red wine to each pound. Add salt, freshly ground pepper, a pinch of sugar, and a knob of butter. Cook rapidly until the artichokes are tender and the wine reduced to a syrup. Very good with lamb.

Artichokes with Parsley, Garlic and Bacon

Leave the artichokes whole. Cut 2 oz bacon (for each pound) into cubes and cook in a frying-pan for a minute or to; add the artichokes, lower the heat, cover the pan and cook gently until tender. Sprinkle with chopped parsley and garlic and freshly ground black pepper.

Artichokes with Gruyère and Cream

1 lb artichokes,
   parboiled and peeled
¼ pint thick cream

Salt, pepper
3 oz grated Gruyère

Cut the artichokes into thick slices or cubes and finish cooking them in the cream. Stir in half the cheese and check seasoning. Pour into a *gratin* dish, sprinkle with the rest of the cheese and brown under the grill. Serve on its own, with plenty of brown bread.

AUBERGINES

This good-tempered and versatile vegetable is now a fairly common sight in August and September in even the smallest market town. It will mix well with most of the other seasonal vegetables, and as part of a *ratatouille* or *brouillade* will keep hot or reheat quite happily. Like courgettes, they should be sliced, lightly salted and left to drain for an hour or so before cooking to remove excess liquid and bitterness.

Brouillade d'Aubergines

1 lb sliced, unpeeled aubergines	2 cloves garlic, chopped
2 tblsps olive oil	4 large tomatoes, skinned
1 large onion, chopped	Salt and pepper
	Fresh basil

Salt the aubergines and put them to drain in a colander with a plate on top for an hour. Heat the olive oil in a heavy saucepan and add the onion, garlic and aubergines. Stir well, lower the heat, cover and cook gently for 20 minutes. Chop the tomatoes roughly and add them to the pan; remove the lid and simmer until the tomato juices have all but evaporated and the vegetables are mushy. Stir in salt and pepper to taste, and about 1 tablespoon chopped fresh basil. This freezes well, and is delicious with sausages.

Aubergine Fritters

1 lb aubergines	1 quartered lemon

Batter:

4 oz flour	¼ pint warm water
½ teasp salt	Stiffly beaten egg white
1 egg yolk	

Sift the flour and salt into a bowl, and break the egg yolk into the middle. Add the water gradually, beating hard, until you have a smooth batter. Leave it to stand while the sliced and salted aubergines drain. Beat the egg white and fold it into the batter. Dry the slices of aubergine on paper towels, dip them in the batter and fry in deep, hot, oil for about 3-5 minutes, until golden. Drain on more paper towels and serve with sea salt and lemon quarters.

Cold Stuffed Aubergines

4 medium aubergines
2 large tomatoes, skinned
   and chopped
6 oz cooked rice

1 small onion
2 cloves garlic
Freshly ground coriander
Salt and pepper

For the sauce:

1 lb skinned and chopped
   tomatoes
Salt and pepper

Basil
Olive oil

Cut the aubergines in half lengthways, scoop out the seeds, sprinkle with salt and leave upside down for an hour to drain. Combine the rest of the ingredients, chopping the onion and garlic, and stuff the aubergines with this mixture. Heat the olive oil in a large fireproof dish and put the aubergines into it. Arrange the chopped tomatoes, mixed with the basil, salt and pepper, around the aubergines and cover with foil. Bake gently at 325° F for about 45 minutes, or until done. Remove the foil and brown the tops. Leave to cool.

BROAD BEANS

Broad Bean Tops

If you grow your own beans and are pinching out the tops to discourage black-fly.

1 lb tops, well washed
Salt and black pepper

Butter

Bring a little salted water to the boil, throw in the tops and cook fast, without a lid, until tender – about 5 minutes. Drain them well in a colander. Melt a little butter in the hot saucepan, return the tops to it and shake the pan gently. Season with black pepper and serve with grilled pork chops.

Young Broad Beans, Whole

Again, if you grow your own and have a large crop. Pick the beans when they are a finger's length and cook them as you would French beans. Serve with butter and a squeeze of lemon juice.

Broad Beans with Butter, Parsley and Garlic

1½ lb elderly broad beans,
    shelled
2 oz butter

2 tblsps chopped parsley
½ clove garlic chopped

Cook the beans until barely tender, drain them and leave them to cool. When they are cool enough to handle, remove the tough skins. A squeeze at one end is enough for them to slip out easily. Reheat in the butter, garlic and parsley.

Broad Beans with Artichokes

(*See page* 120)

Broad Bean Pod Purée

This freezes well, and is very good with ham and salt pork dishes For a stiffer purée, mix it with a little mashed potato. Cook the pods (reserve the beans themselves for another dish) in salted water until tender, drain them and put them through the vegetable-mill; season the purée with a little butter or thick cream, salt and pepper.

FRENCH BEANS

Best straight from the garden, with melted butter with a few bread-crumbs stirred in. Be careful not to overcook or keep hot.

French Bean Salad

1 lb beans
French dressing (½ tblsp lemon
  juice, 3 tblsps olive oil,

salt, freshly ground black
  pepper)
1 teasp crushed coriander seeds

Cook the beans until just tender. Drain and mix with the dressing while they are still warm. Sprinkle with the crushed coriander seeds, and allow to cool. Very good with cold ham.

RUNNER BEANS

Don't shred runner beans – this only means that you end up with a pile of something like boiled hay. If the beans are very large, don't buy them. If growing your own, pick them when they are about 6 inches long, top and tail them and cook them whole. If longer than that, string them with one of those potato peelers with a revolving blade and then break them into large pieces.

Runner Beans with Cream and Onion

1 lb medium runner beans
1 small onion
1 oz butter

3-4 tblsps thick cream
Salt and pepper

Cook the chopped onion in butter until soft. Top and tail the beans, string them, if necessary, and break into pieces. Cook them until just tender in boiling water with the lid off. Mix them with the onions. Stir in the cream and boil fast until the cream thickens. Check the seasoning and serve, perhaps with roast chicken.

BEETROOT

When possible, buy beetroot with the leaves on (make sure they are fresh); you will then have three separate vegetables:

Beetroot Leaves

Remove the central rib and wash carefully. Cook as you would spinach, with only the water that remains on the leaves after washing. Serve with a squeeze of orange juice.

Beetroot Stalks

The ribs you removed from the leaves. Cook in boiling water until tender. Drain and return to the pan; add a knob of butter and some freshly-ground black pepper, slicing them across once or twice with a sharp knife.

The Beetroot Itself

Twist off the leaves, scrub the beetroot and boil until tender. This depends on their size; small ones take about an hour, and a pressure cooker is a great help. Alternatively, bake them in a low oven, if you have it on for some other reason – they will have more flavour. When they are cooked, remove the skins, chop or slice them and reheat a) with butter and a few caraway seeds; b) with orange juice and a little grated rind; c) with chopped garlic and butter; d) with sour cream and crushed coriander; e) serve as a salad (*see* page 54).

BROCCOLI

The first of the season's crop, whether bought or home grown, only needs melted butter. Later on, when it becomes tougher, more elaborate recipes are needed.

Broccoli with White Wine and Garlic

1 lb broccoli
2 tblsps olive oil
Scrap chopped garlic

Salt and pepper
1 glass white wine

Wash the broccoli, and drain it. Split any thick stalks so that they cook in the same time as the thin ones. Cook the garlic in the oil, then add the broccoli and a little salt. Turn it in the oil, then pour on the wine, cover and simmer until the broccoli is tender. Remove the lid, reduce the wine a little, season with black pepper and serve very hot.

Broccoli with Cheese

3 tblsps garlic cream cheese
  (Boursin, or home-made)

1 lb broccoli
3 tblsps grated Cheddar

Cook the broccoli until just tender in boiling water, without a lid. Drain and return to the pan to dry. Add the cream cheese and let it melt, stirring carefully to coat the broccoli but being careful not to break it up too much. Turn into a warmed *gratin* dish, spread with the grated Cheddar and brown quickly under a preheated hot grill.

BRUSSELS SPROUTS

Remove the outer leaves and cut a cross across the base of each stalk with a sharp knife. Cook rapidly in boiling salted water without a lid on the pan, for 10-15 minutes until just tender. They are even better if slightly underdone. Drain thoroughly then return them to the pan to dry off. Add lots of butter and freshly ground pepper, and a squeeze of lemon unless they were fresh from the garden.

Brussels Sprouts with Chestnuts

For each pound of sprouts allow at least ½ pound chestnuts. Make a cut on the rounded side of each chestnut, then cook them in boiling water for 15 minutes. Drain and peel them as soon as they are cool enough to handle. Cook the sprouts as above. Add the chopped chestnuts as they dry in the pan, then stir in a tablespoon of cream. Season to taste and keep warm for about 10 minutes for the flavours to blend.

CABBAGE

The white or Dutch cabbage is ideal for salads, or for making sauerkraut (shred the cabbage finely, pack it into a jar with some salt, and leave it to ferment, with a weight on top, in a cool place, for a month). I prefer to use the green or Savoy cabbages for hot vegetables.

Cabbage with Mustard and Cream

1 Savoy cabbage	¼ pint single cream
2 oz butter	1 dstsp Meaux mustard

Slice the cabbage finely, discarding any large pieces of stalk. Melt the butter in a heavy pan and cook the cabbage in it, stirring frequently, until tender. Add the cream, raise the heat and cook fast. Stir in the mustard, and when the cream is thick, serve at once.

Stuffed Cabbage

1 Savoy cabbage	Handful of sultanas
1 large chopped onion	Salt and pepper
1 cup rice	A pinch of mixed spice
6-8 oz cold chopped lamb	Strong stock

Wash the cabbage, remove any tatty outer leaves, but leave it whole. Bring a large saucepan of salty water to the boil and blanch the cabbage in it, stalk up, for 10 minutes. Leave to drain, also stalk up, while you prepare the stuffing. Soften the onion in a little oil, then stir in the rice, meat, sultanas and seasoning. Open out the leaves of the cabbage and tuck spoonfuls of the stuffing well down amongst the leaves. Tie the cabbage with tape and fit it into a stoneware casserole. Heat the stock and pour in enough to cover the cabbage by about ½″ (the rice will absorb a lot). Cover with a butter paper and the lid and leave in the oven all day (or for at least 3 hours at 300° F). Serve from the pot.

Red Cabbage

1 large red cabbage	¼ pint red wine
1 large onion	2 oz brown sugar
2 large apples, Cox's or	1 teasp mixed spice
Bramley's	Pepper, pinch salt
Dripping	2 strips orange peel

Slice the onion and apple (if using Cox's remove the cores but don't peel them), and soften them in 2-3 tablespoons goose, duck or pork dripping. Slice the cabbage, removing the central stalk. Add it to the pan with the wine, and as it cooks down, stir in the sugar, spice, pepper and salt. Finally, bury the orange peel, cover the pan tightly and cook very slowly for at least 2 hours, either in or on the stove. This will freeze and reheat without damage, so it is worth making in large quantities. It is delicious with all game.

CARROTS

Lancashire Chopped Carrots and Turnips

½ lb carrots, scraped and sliced	Salt and black pepper
	Slices of toast and dripping
½ lb turnips, scraped and sliced	Gravy from a stew

Cook the carrots and turnips together in boiling salted water until tender. Drain them well and return them to the pan. As they dry, chop them finely with a sharp knife – do not mash them. Season with a little pepper and extra salt if necessary and serve them as they are, piled on slices of toast and dripping, with the gravy poured over them. A lovely winter dish for high tea.

Raw Carrot Salad

(*See page 55*)

Carrots and Rice

A Persian dish, good hot or cold.

1 lb carrots – left whole if very young, or cut into quarters lengthwise if old
1 tblsp olive oil
1 crushed clove garlic

1 oz rice
Lemon juice
Salt and pepper
Chopped chervil

Cook the carrots very gently in the oil, with the garlic, for about 10 minutes. Stir in the rice, so that each grain is coated with oil. Add enough water to cover, bring to the boil and simmer until it has been absorbed by the rice. Cover the pan with a folded cloth and the lid, lower the heat and cook gently until both carrots and rice are tender – about 20 minutes. Squeeze some lemon juice over the rice, add salt and freshly ground pepper and a dusting of chopped chervil. Hot, it is delicious with roast lamb or veal; cold, it can be served as an *hors d'oeuvre*.

CAULIFLOWER

Sicilian Cauliflower

Very unusual, filling and good.

1 cauliflower
2 large chopped onions
2 cloves garlic, chopped
3 oz stoned sliced black olives

6 chopped anchovy fillets
6 tblsps olive oil
2 oz grated mature Cheddar
½ pint red wine

Separate the cauliflower into flowerets, wash and dry them. Oil the bottom of a heavy casserole, and put in a layer of chopped onion, garlic, olives and anchovies; cover with a layer of cauliflower, sprinkled with a little olive oil, then add a layer of cheese. Continue in this order until the ingredients are used up, finishing with a layer of cheese. Pour in the wine, put on the lid and cook on top of the stove, or in the oven, for about 40 minutes, or until the cauliflower is tender. Remove the lid and raise the heat to evaporate some of the wine. Serve it from the casserole with hot garlic bread.

Cauliflower Vinaigrette

Dress slightly undercooked cauliflower while it is still warm with a vinaigrette to which you have added a chopped hard-boiled egg. Garnish with raw onion rings.

CELERIAC

Celeriac is just beginning to be seen north of London, though often only in expensive greengrocers at ludicrously high prices. I don't know why it is regarded with such suspicion as its flavour is hardly alarming – celery with undertones of turnip perhaps best describes it.

Roast Celeriac

1 large celeriac root   2 tblsps beef dripping
Squeeze of lemon juice

Peel the celeriac, cut it into large chunks and parboil it in salted water to which you have added the lemon juice (it discolours easily). When it is still firm, drain it well. Melt the dripping in a *gratin* dish and turn the pieces of celeriac in it until covered with fat. Roast it in a hot oven for 35-40 minutes. Best of all, roast it round a piece of beef.

Celeriac Purée

Cook equal quantities of celeriac and potatoes in water until tender. Drain them and put them through the vegetable-mill; beat in plenty of hot milk, butter, salt and pepper, and a tablespoon of chopped celery leaves.

Celeriac Salad

Grate or chop finely a peeled celeriac root (best of all, put it through the shredding disk on a *mouli-juliénne*). Squeeze some lemon juice over it and mix well to stop it from going brown. Mix about ½ teacup home-made mayonnaise with enough thin cream or top-of-the-milk to make it easy to blend with the celeriac. Season with salt, black pepper and chopped parsley.

CELERY

Best in winter, when it is sold crisp and white under a coating of fine black soil, after a week or so of early frost. Clean green celery in polythene bags is not the same.

Braised Celery with White Wine

1 head celery	1 large glass white wine
3 oz butter	Salt, pepper

Separate the stalks, scrub them well and remove any strings from the outside ones. Cut into 2″ lengths. Melt the butter in a heavy pan and stir the celery into it, together with a little salt and pepper. Pour in the wine, boil fast for a few seconds, then lower the heat, cover the pan and cook gently until the celery is just tender. Evaporate some of the wine if necessary, check the seasoning and serve.

Celery, Apple and Walnut Salad

6 sticks celery, sliced	Dressing made with lemon
2 Cox's apples, cored, sliced, but not peeled	juice, olive oil and a little salt
2 tblsps chopped walnuts	

Mix all the ingredients and serve at once.

CHICORY

This dish is a meal on its own, to be made with the white forced chicory. Home-grown 'Sugarloaf' chicory is not really suitable.

8 heads chicory	1 oz grated cheese
8 large slices ham	1 oz breadcrumbs
¾ pint well-flavoured cheese *béchamel*, seasoned with 1 teasp Meaux mustard	1 oz butter

Blanch the heads of chicory for 5 minutes in boiling salted water; drain well and wrap each in a slice of ham. Pour enough sauce into a large *gratin* dish to cover the bottom; arrange the ham-wrapped chicory on top, and pour on the rest of the sauce. Distribute the cheese, breadcrumbs, and butter cut into small pieces, over the top and bake for 30 minutes at 375° F, until golden brown and bubbling.

Chicory Salad with Walnuts and Chicken Livers

(See page 55)

COURGETTES

These are worth growing yourself if you have the space, as you can cook the flowers as well as the courgettes themselves.

Courgette Flower Fritters

Inspect each flower inside for earwigs, then dip them straight into batter (see recipe on page 122), then into hot, deep oil and fry for 2-3 minutes. Serve immediately.

Stuffed Courgette Flowers

Using the stuffing for aubergines on page 123, gently put a couple of teaspoons into each flower, folding the petals over to make a neat parcel. Run a film of olive oil over the bottom of a casserole, pack the flowers into it, add a very little light stock and cook, covered, for about 20 minutes. Serve cold, with extra lemon juice squeezed over them.

Courgettes Baked with Garlic and Herbs

2 lb courgettes	chervil, parsley, tarragon,
2 cloves garlic,	marjoram, chives, fennel
cut into slivers	Olive oil
4 tblsps chopped fresh herbs –	Salt, pepper

Halve the courgettes lengthwise, rub the cut sides with salt and leave to drain, cut sides down, for an hour. Make small slits all over each half and put a sliver of garlic into each one. Scatter the herbs over the courgettes, season with salt and freshly ground black pepper, put a teaspoon of oil on top of each half and bake, in a baking tin, at 325° F, for 45 minutes to one hour. Good hot or cold.

CUCUMBERS

'To stew cucumbers. From the Devil Tavern, Fleet Street. Take a dozen large green Cucumbers, that are not too full of Seeds; pare them, and slice them; then take two large Onions, and shred them indifferently small. Put these in a Sauce-pan, and set them over the Fire to stew, with as much Salt as you think convenient; stir them now and then till they are tender, and then pour them into a Cullender to drain from the Water, and are as dry as possible you can make them; then flour them, and put some Pepper to them. After this, burn some Butter in a Frying-pan, and when it is very hot, put in your Cucumbers, and stir them continually till they are brown; then put to them about a Gill of Red-port; and when that is well mixed with them, serve them hot, under roast Mutton, or Lamb; or else serve them on a Plate, upon Sippets fried or dipped in strong Beef Gravy.' Richard Bradley, *The Country Housewife*, 1753.

A very good 18th century recipe; let the butter turn brown, rather than burn, before you put the cucumbers in the frying-pan.

Cacik or Tsatsiki

A cucumber and yoghourt salad.

1 cucumber, peeled
½ pint yoghourt
2 cloves garlic

2-3 teasps chopped fresh mint
Salt and pepper

Chop the cucumber finely, sprinkle it with salt and leave it to drain for an hour in a colander with a plate on top. Mix it into the yoghourt, together with the garlic (also finely chopped), the mint, freshly ground black pepper, and extra salt if necessary. Serve very cold, decorated with whole mint leaves.

LEEKS

Leeks Baked with Red Wine

1 lb leeks
A little butter

A large glass red wine
Salt and pepper

Trim off the green leaves and leave the white part whole. Heat about 1 oz butter in a heavy casserole, and turn the leeks over in this once or twice before pouring on the red wine; add salt and freshly-ground pepper, bring the wine to the boil, then cover the pan and cook the leeks in a moderate (350° F) oven for about 45 minutes. Reduce the wine a little at the end if there is a lot left.

Leeks Baked in Cream

1 lb leeks, prepared as in the
   preceding recipe
2 oz butter

Salt, pepper, nutmeg
1 teasp flour
¼ pint thick cream

Put the leeks into a *gratin* dish with the melted butter; season with salt, pepper and freshly grated nutmeg. Mix the flour with a little of the cream, then into the rest of the cream, before pouring it over the leeks. Cover the dish with a foil lid and bake in a moderate oven until the leeks are tender (about 45 minutes at 350° F). Remove the foil and continue to cook until the cream bubbles and thickens. Check the seasoning and serve, perhaps with boiled ham.

Leeks can be served *à la grecque* as in the recipe on page 53, and can be used instead of chicory in the ham and chicory dish on page 133.

MUSHROOMS

Mushrooms with Parsley and Tarragon

½ lb mushrooms
1 oz butter
1 tblsp chopped parsley

1 tblsp chopped tarragon
Scrap chopped garlic
Salt and pepper

Wipe (never peel) the mushrooms, and leaving the stalks on, quarter them. Cook them gently in the butter until they begin to give out their juices, then stir in the herbs and garlic. Season with a very little salt, and pepper. This is particularly good as a supper dish with baked potatoes. Halve the cooked potatoes, mash the centres with a fork, and put a spoonful or two of the mushrooms into each one.

Raw Mushroom and Fennel Salad

½ lb firm white mushrooms
1 head Italian fennel
Sea salt

Lemon juice
Olive oil
Black pepper

Wipe and quarter the mushrooms and slice the fennel. Put them both into a bowl, season with the salt and pepper and lemon juice, and stir in enough olive oil to moisten the salad. This salad is very good on its own as a first course, or served with cold chicken or turkey.

Mushrooms à la Grecque

(*See page 53*)

ONIONS

Baked Onions

1 lb English onions –
the largest you can find

Butter
Salt and pepper

Wash the onions and leave them whole. Put them on a greased baking sheet and bake for 1½ hours at 350° F, or until tender. Cut off the tops and fork butter, salt and pepper into the centre of each. Baked onions are not only delicious, but are good cures for colds, insomnia and hangovers.

Baked Onions with Red Wine

1 lb small onions
2 tblsps olive oil

½ pint red wine (approx)
Salt and pepper

Peel the onions; heat the oil in a casserole in which the onions will just fit in one layer, and brown the onions all over in it. Heat the wine, season with salt and plenty of freshly-ground pepper, and pour it round the onions – it should come half way up them. Bake, uncovered, in a low oven for about one hour, or until the onions are tender. You can use a medium dry white wine instead of red if you want to serve this dish with white meat.

Yorkshire Ploughman's Salad

(Sometimes called Yorkshire Ploughboy)

3 large onions
¼ of a red cabbage
1 tblsp treacle

2 tblsps vinegar
Pepper and salt

Shred the onions and cabbage finely and mix with the treacle, vinegar, pepper and little salt. As Eliza Acton says 'This, though certainly not a very refined order of salad, is scarcely so unpalatable as such ingredients would seem to promise.' Her own recipe uses lettuce, which is not as good as the cabbage version; the onions are the main ingredient. Very good with cold salt beef.

PARSNIPS

Roast parsnips with beef, following the directions for roast celeriac on page 131, or serve them in thick slices, coated in butter and parsley, with homely toad-in-the-hole. Parsnip soup, flavoured with a little curry powder is one of the best winter soups, and some parsnip should be included in any winter soup. Parsnip and potato purée goes well with game, and is also good with lamb. Salt cod, egg sauce and boiled parsnips is a traditional Lenten dish, but a better variation is to bake fresh haddock in parsnip sauce:

Parsnip Sauce

1 lb parsnips	¼ pint single cream
1 oz butter	2 hard boiled eggs
1 oz flour	Salt, pepper, nutmeg

Peel and slice the parsnips and cook in boiling salted water until tender. Put them through the vegetable-mill. Melt the butter and stir in the flour, beat in the parsnip purée, cook gently for 15 minutes, then add the cream and season to taste. Pour this sauce over 1 lb fresh haddock fillet rolled in salt, pepper, chopped parsley and a little lemon juice, surrounded by the quartered eggs. Sprinkle breadcrumbs over the top and bake for 30 minutes at 375° F.

PEAS

The first young peas are best if picked, shelled, cooked and eaten within half-an-hour, but of course this is only possible if you grow your own. If your timetable dictates podding the peas some time in advance, shell them into a basin and cover with a layer of empty pods to keep them moist until you can cook them. As peas age, you can cook them more elaborately. This is Elizabeth Raffald's recipe, dated 1769:

To Stew Peas with Lettuces

'Shell your peas, boil them in hard water, with salt in it, drain them in a sieve, then cut your lettuces in slices, and fry them in fresh butter, put your peas and lettuces into a tossing-pan, with a little good gravy, pepper and salt, thicken it with flour and butter, put in a little shred mint, and serve it up in a soup dish.'

Sformato di Piselli

An Italian steamed pea soufflé, usually served with a sauce of some kind. It can be made with any vegetable – spinach is particularly good – but fresh (or frozen) peas make the best *sformato*.

2 lb shelled peas	¼ pint good stock
(about 3 lb in their pods)	3 eggs
1 small onion	Salt and pepper
1 oz butter	Nutmeg
1 oz flour	

Chop the onion and cook it with the peas in salted boiling water until both are tender. Drain and put them through the vegetable-mill, reserving a few whole peas for the sauce. Make a *béchamel* with the butter, flour and stock – it should be very thick, as though for a normal soufflé. Off the heat, beat in the pea purée, then the egg yolks. Check the seasoning, and flavour with a little nutmeg. Butter a ring mould, or hinged cake tin, very thoroughly, and stand it in a baking tin with water to come halfway up the sides. Heat the oven to 325° F. Whip the egg whites stiffly and fold them into the pea mixture, then pour it into the mould. Cover the top with greaseproof paper and bake for 45-50 minutes until set. You can now turn it out and put your ready-prepared sauce into the centre, if you used a ring mould, or poured round and over it if you used a cake tin. A *béchamel* made with ham stock, cubes of ham, the whole reserved peas and 2-3 tablespoons of cream stirred in makes a suitable sauce for this *sformato di piselli*. An ordinary Bolognese sauce is delicious with a spinach *sformato*.

SWEET PEPPERS

Stuffed Peppers

6 medium-sized peppers	1 lb raw minced lamb
(choose 2 red, 2 green	2 tblsps tomato purée
and 2 yellow if possible)	2 oz chopped almonds
1 large onion	Salt, pepper, oregano
Olive oil	12 cloves garlic

Halve the peppers lengthwise and remove the white pith and the seeds. Chop the onion, cook it in a couple of tablespoons of olive oil until soft, then add the lamb. Raise the heat to seal it, then stir in the tomato purée, the almonds, salt, freshly ground pepper and oregano. Stuff each pepper-half with this mixture. Peel the garlic, crush it slightly, then bury one clove in the stuffing of each pepper. Oil a baking tin and arrange the peppers in it, cover with butter papers and bake in a moderate oven (350° F) until the peppers are soft – about 45 minutes to 1 hour.

Pepe Maria

6 tblsps olive oil	1 clove garlic
½ tblsp red wine vinegar	8 walnut halves
1 tblsp Dijon mustard	4 peppers
Salt	8 anchovy fillets
Black pepper	

Make a dressing with the oil, vinegar, mustard, plenty of salt and pepper, and the roughly chopped walnuts and garlic. Put the peppers under a hot grill, turning frequently, until the skin blisters and can be removed with a sharp knife. Cut them in half to remove the pith and seeds, then into strips. Mix them, while still warm, into the dressing, add the whole anchovy fillets, and allow to cool before serving as part of an *hors d'oeuvre*.

POTATOES

The Irish Way to Boil Potatoes in Their Skins

Try to choose potatoes which are roughly the same size. Scrub them, then fit them in one layer in a large saucepan. Cover them with cold water, bring it to the boil and add 3 teasps salt. Simmer until the potatoes are nearly cooked, then raise the heat and boil fast until they are done. Drain them and return them to the pan to dry off over a gentle heat. The skins should split to reveal the floury interiors. Do not put a lid on them again before you serve them – not even on the serving dish.

The Lancashire Way to Boil Potatoes

Remove the peel as thinly as possible (Prestige make a potato peeler with a revolving blade which is very good for peeling thinly) and leave the potatoes to soak in *very* salty cold water for an hour or two. Put them into a saucepan with fresh water and add another generous quantity of salt (in the old days, sea-water was used). Boil until nearly done; add a little cold water toward the end to lower the heat and make the potatoes floury. Drain well, return to the pan and cover with a folded cloth and finish cooking on a low heat. This means that quite a lot of potato will stick to the pan. Scrape it off and serve it with the rest, it has a particularly delicious, slightly scorched flavour. Soak the pan overnight in cold water.

Pommes de Terre à l'Ardennaise

I first tasted their dish in the Ardennes, where it is served with venison or boar.

1½ lb potatoes	6 juniper berries
(Desirée are a good variety for this dish)	1 clove garlic
	2 teasps salt
3 oz butter	Freshly-ground pepper
1 tblsp olive oil	

Shred the potatoes by putting them through a *mouli-juliénne,* or grating them on a cheese grater. Soak them in a bowl of cold water for about 30 minutes to get rid of the starch, drain them well and dry them in a tea-cloth. Melt the butter and oil in a frying-pan, crush the juniper berries, garlic and salt together and add them to the pan. Put in the potatoes and mix them gently with the butter and seasonings. Cover with a foil lid and cook gently until they are soft, with a golden crust on the bottom. This version is good with game; with lamb, use rosemary instead of juniper; and with beef, use thyme.

SALSIFY

This curious root vegetable sometimes called the Vegetable Oyster because of its faint fishy flavour, seems to be coming back into favour. It is best served on its own, so that its subtle taste can be appreciated.

Scrub the salsify, boil it until tender, then remove the skins. Cut each root into thick slices. These can now be finished off in butter, to which you can add parsley, a very little garlic, and a squeeze of lemon juice, or you can dip them into the batter on page 122, and fry them in deep hot oil.

SPINACH

There is a way of cooking spinach which will convert even the most decided spinach-hater; it is a dish worth waiting for:

Seven Day Buttered Spinach

| 2-3 lb spinach | 12 oz unsalted butter |
| Salt, pepper, nutmeg | Orange quarters |

Remove the central rib and wash the leaves thoroughly. Pack the wet spinach into a heavy pan, without any extra water, and cook it over a moderate heat until you can cut it with a wooden spoon. Drain it thoroughly and chop it through once or twice with a sharp knife. Return it to the pan with an ounce or two of the butter and put it over a low heat until the spinach has absorbed the butter. Transfer it to a basin, cover it and keep it in the fridge. Next day, reheat it with a bit more of the butter, then return it to the fridge; repeat this every day for the next five days. On the seventh day, plan a good lunch to accompany the spinach – a large piece of gammon, or a succulent roast chicken. Reheat the spinach for the last time. Check the seasoning – it will probably need salt, black pepper and a little nutmeg. Put it in a hot dish and surround it with orange quarters; spinach and orange go extraordinarily well together.

TOMATOES

I never buy tomatoes in the winter, preferring to forgo fresh, but flavourless, tomato salads in favour of dishes which use the Italian tinned tomatoes.

Stuffed Tomatoes with Olives

8 large tomatoes	1-2 cloves garlic
4 slices wholemeal bread	6 stoned black olives
1 teasp green peppercorns	2-3 tblsps olive oil
Fresh basil and parsley	Salt

Cut the tomatoes in half, score the cut surfaces and rub with salt. Put upside down on a plate to drain for half-an-hour. Remove the crusts from the bread and cut into cubes. Put these, the peppercorns, garlic, herbs and stoned olives into the blender and blend until finely chopped. Moisten with the olive oil; scoop the insides from the tomatoes and mix with the breadcrumbs and other ingredients, checking to see if more salt is necessary. Stuff the tomatoes with this mixture, arrange in an ovenproof dish and cook for about 30 minutes at 350° F. Good hot or cold.

Tomato Risotto

Approx 2 pints chicken stock	1 lb tomatoes,
2 oz butter	skinned and chopped
1 medium onion	Chopped fresh basil and
2 cloves garlic	marjoram
12 oz Italian rice	Salt, pepper

Put the stock in a saucepan and keep it simmering over a low heat. Melt the butter and cook the onion and garlic in it until soft; add the rice, stir it well. Then pour on about ½ pint of the hot stock. Simmer until the stock is absorbed, then pour in another ½ pint. Continue adding stock in this way until the rice is tender but not soft (*al dente*). Add the chopped tomatoes, the herbs and a little salt and black pepper, and leave over a low heat until the tomatoes are hot but not cooked – they should keep their fresh flavour. This risotto should be rather liquid; serve plenty of butter and grated Parmesan with it.

TURNIPS

Turnips are delicious when eaten very young. Older ones with a stronger flavour are best for the following recipe:

Punch-Nep

A Welsh dish, very good with the lamb on page 89.

1 lb potatoes
1 lb white turnips
Salt and pepper

About ¼ pint single cream
or 3 oz melted butter

Peel, cook and mash the two vegetables separately, with a little butter. Mix them together, beating hard, then season generously. Transfer the purée to a warm vegetable dish, smooth the top, then make small holes all over the surface with the handle of a wooden spoon. Fill each hole with the heated cream, or melted butter. Cream is best.

Young Turnips with Bacon

1 lb small, young turnips
2-3 oz bacon, cut in strips

Pepper and salt
Chopped parsley

Peel the turnip and cut them into quarters. Cook them in boiling salted water until tender. Drain well. Melt a little butter in a frying-pan and cook the bacon in it for about 5 minutes; add the turnip quarters and continue cooking until the bacon is crisp and the turnips are beginning to brown. Season and sprinkle with parsley before serving.

WATERCRESS

It is sad that watercress is now regarded primarily as a garnish; in the 18th century it was a favourite salad, its richness in iron recognized as a valuable purifier of the blood, especially after a long winter on a diet of salted meat and root vegetables. Not for nothing do the French call watercress soup 'Potage Santé'. But watercress is delicious, as well as being good for you, and makes one of the best winter salads, its rich greenness often very welcome after a substantial meat course.

Watercress Salad

4 oz watercress
 (or 1 large bunch)
Dressing made with lemon
juice, olive oil and a
little salt

Remove the tough, lower stalks and wash the sprigs of watercress, draining them in a lettuce basket. Toss them in the dressing just before you are ready to eat the salad, as, like lettuce, watercress quickly goes limp and soggy. There are several good variations to this basic salad:

Watercress Salad with Oranges

Peel and slice 2 oranges, making sure you get rid of as much of the pith as possible. Make the dressing with wine vinegar instead of lemon juice, and stir the orange slices into it some time before you add the watercress. This salad goes very well with the spiced duck on page 111.

Watercress Salad with Potatoes

You will need good waxy potatoes for this; Pink Fir Apple are best, but Desirée will do at a pinch. Boil about 1 lb potatoes in their skins, peel them as soon as you can handle them, and mix them with a generous quantity of dressing while they are still warm. Add the watercress to this potato salad just before serving.

Watercress with Carrots

Add roughly chopped watercress to the carrot salad on page 55, again, just before you are ready to eat.

Watercress Sauce

This sauce is extremely good with trout and with grilled veal chops. You can substitute fresh cream for the sour cream if you prefer.

1 large bunch watercress   2-3 tblsps stock
¼ pint sour cream   Salt, a little pepper

Keeping back a few whole leaves, put the rest of the bunch in the blender with enough stock to make a pulp. Put this pulp through a sieve into the cream and mix well. Check the seasoning, and serve chilled.

Watercress and Anchovy Butter

The leaves from a small   2-3 teasps anchovy essence
   bunch of watercress   A little lemon juice
4 oz softened butter

Chop the watercress finely, and blend it into the butter with the anchovy essence. Add a squeeze of lemon, then check the seasoning. Use this for brown-bread sandwiches, or chill and serve it with grilled fish or lamb chops. It is also good as a savoury butter wtih cheese.

· Puddings ·
· Sweet Dishes ·
· Cakes & Biscuits. ·

Puddings, Sweet Dishes, Cakes and Biscuits

Good cheese and fresh fruit are all one has room for after a filling main course, but there are times when a proper pudding is very welcome. English puddings are wonderful but fairly solid, probably because they were always served before the cheese. In France, cheese precedes the dessert – based on the idea that whatever wine accompanied the meat course was suitable to drink with cheese. Dessert, therefore, had to be light and insubstantial. This chapter contains recipes for both sorts of pudding.

Spread-Eagle Pudding

'Cut the Crust off three stale Halfpenny Rolls, and slice them into a Pan; then set three Pints of Milk on the Fire, making it scalding hot, but not to boil; pour it over the Bread, cover it close, and let it stand an Hour; sweeten it with Sugar, add a very little Salt, a Nutmeg grated, a Pound of shred Sewet, half a Pound of Currants, half a Pint of cold Milk, ten Yolks and Five Whites of Eggs; stir it well, butter your Dish, and bake it half an Hour.' Richard Bradley, *The Country Housewife*, 1753.

Bag Pudding

A scaled-down version of the above.

8 oz fresh white breadcrumbs	2 eggs
½ pint milk	1 oz brown sugar
Strip lemon rind	2 oz sultanas
Grated nutmeg	2 oz candied peel
1 oz melted butter	2 tblsps sherry

Scald the milk with the lemon rind and nutmeg and pour it over the breadcrumbs – leave them to soak for an hour. Remove the rind and beat in the rest of the ingredients. You can then pour the mixture into a well-buttered baking dish, or into a roasting-bag, which is preferable as it seems to produce a lighter pudding. Bake for 45-50 minutes at 375° F. Serve with thin cream or brandy butter.

Steamed Jam Pudding

4 oz butter
4 oz vanilla sugar
2 eggs
8 oz home-made jam

4 oz plain flour
½ teasp baking powder
Pinch salt

Sauce:

Juice 2 oranges

6 tblsps jam used for pudding

Beat the butter and sugar until light, then add the eggs and jam (raspberry, strawberry or blackcurrant are all good), beating hard. Sift the flour, baking powder and salt together and fold into the mixture. Pour it into a buttered pudding basin and cover the top with a butter paper, then a foil lid, tied on with string so that you can lift it out of the pan easily. Steam, covered, for 1½ hours, adding more boiling water if necessary. To make the sauce, heat the jam and orange juice together until the jam melts. Turn the pudding on to a warm dish and pour the sauce over it; serve with thin cream. A marmalade version of this pudding is very good too; add only 6 oz to the mixture if you are using a bitter variety.

Sussex Pond Pudding

The very best of all suet puddings.

4 oz plain flour
½ teasp baking powder
Pinch salt
4 oz suet
4 oz fresh breadcrumbs
Milk to mix

4 oz brown sugar
4 oz unsalted butter
Scraping of nutmeg
1 large, thin-skinned juicy
  lemon

Make the suet crust: mix the flour, baking powder, salt, suet and breadcrumbs, adding enough milk to make a soft dough. Roll out into a circle and cut out (as if from a clock) '15 minutes' from that circle. Butter a pudding basin thickly and sprinkle some of the brown sugar round the inside. Fit the '45 minutes' of suet into the basin, joining the two cut edges neatly – you'll find that it fits perfectly. Cut the butter into cubes and mix with the rest of the brown sugar and a little nutmeg; put half into the paste-lined basin. Prick the lemon all over with a carving-fork, so that the flavours can mingle, put it in the basin and cover it with the rest of the butter and sugar. Roll the remaining '15 minutes' of pastry into a circle and fit it on top of the pudding, pinching top and bottom together with wet fingers. Put a butter paper loosely on top, then fit on a foil lid, tied with string. Lower the basin into a saucepan of boiling water (checking that the water doesn't bubble over the top of the basin) and steam, covered, for 3 hours. Loosen the pudding with a knife, then turn it out on to a hot plate – the sugar and butter will have turned into a sort of caramel sauce, the lemon will be soft and slightly sweetened and quite delicious. Cream is superfluous, but should be there for the greedy.

Le Groseilleat

A filling tart-cum-pie.

Pastry:

12 oz plain flour
2 oz ground almonds
6 oz vanilla sugar
4 oz soft butter
2 oz lard

1 whole egg plus 1 yolk
A little cold water

3 tblsps thick cream

Filling:

1½ lb gooseberries
1 head elderflowers
3 oz sugar
¼ pint water

½ lb redcurrants
1 oz sugar
2 tblsps water

Mix the flour and ground almonds and make a well in the centre. Put the sugar, beaten egg plus yolk, the butter and lard cut into small pieces into the middle. With the electric beater at a very slow speed, blend all together until you have a smooth paste, adding a little cold water if the eggs are small. The less the pastry is handled the better; wrap it in greaseproof paper and put it in the fridge while you prepare the filling.

Top and tail the gooseberries; make a syrup from the elderflowers, sugar and water. Poach the gooseberries gently in this until they are tender. Cool, then drain. Make a syrup from the rest of the sugar and water and cook the redcurrants, their stalks removed, in this until they have a jam-like consistency, reducing the syrup if necessary.

Line a large flan tin with a removable base, with ⅔ of the pastry. Do not roll it out; simply ease the paste over the base and right up the sides with your hands, patching any tears. Line the pastry with foil, pressed down firmly, and bake for 10-15 minutes at 450° F. Remove the foil and return the flan to the oven for a further 10 minutes.

Put the drained gooseberries in the flan case and spread the redcurrants over the top. Roll the remaining pastry into a circle to fit the tin, and cut a circle about 2 in in diameter out of the middle. Fit gently on top of the redcurrants. Brush with egg-white and dust with caster sugar. Bake for 25-30 minutes at 400° F until the top is golden. Serve it warm, not hot, with the cream poured in through the hold in the lid just before serving.

This can be made in the winter by using frozen or bottled gooseberries in elderflower syrup (*see* page 159) and redcurrant jelly.

Tortoiseshell Apple Flan

8 oz shortcrust pastry   1 orange
½ pint apple purée   2 tblsps water
2 tblsps marmalade   2 oz caster sugar
1 tblsp vanilla sugar

Line a greased flan tin with the pastry and bake blind, as above. Put the marmalade, apple purée and sugar into a liquidizer and blend. Taste to see if more sugar is needed, then fill the flan case with the mixture. Peel the orange and slice it thinly, removing all pips and as much pith as possible. Arrange the orange slices over the surface of the purée. Make some caramel by dissolving 2 oz of sugar in 2 tblsps of water, and then boiling fast until it turns mahogany colour. Pour it carefully over the orange slices, without covering them entirely, to give a tortoiseshell effect. Do not do this too long in advance or the caramel will soften. The idea is to make a crisp cover for the purée. Serve with whipped cream.

Praline Oranges

6 oranges   6 oz caster sugar
2 oz blanched almonds   6 tblsps water

Peel the oranges, removing as much pith as you can, then slice them thinly. Arrange them in a shallow dish and leave to stand for an hour or so. About 1 hour before serving, drain the juice from the oranges into a saucepan and add the caster sugar and water. Heat gently to dissolve the sugar. Chop the almonds coarsely, add them to the sugar and water, then boil fast until it caramelizes. Pour this quickly over the orange slices.

Baked Pears and Blackberries

2 lb hard pears   ¼ pint water
1½ lb blackberries   4 cloves
   (wild, preferably)   2 in cinnamon stick
¼ pint port or red wine   4 tblsps brown sugar

Peel the pears, keeping them whole and leaving their stalks on. Cut a small piece off the bottom of each so that they will stand upright. Stand them up in a deep stoneware casserole, pour on the port or wine, and water, and add the blackberries, sugar and spices. Cook in the lowest possible oven until the pears are tender and brownish-red, basting them as the liquid evaporates. Arrange them in a dish which will complement their beautiful colour. Reduce the syrup a little and pour it round the pears. The blackberries will have become jam. Serve cold, with cinnamon-flavoured whipped cream.

Blackcurrant-Leaf Sorbet

Approx 2 oz young blackcurrant leaves	10 oz caster sugar
	Juice 2 lemons
1 pint water	2 egg whites

Dissolve the sugar in the water over a low heat, then boil fast for 5 minutes to produce a syrup. Add the washed and torn-up leaves, stir well, cover the pan and leave to infuse for about ½ hour, or until the syrup is well-flavoured. Stir in the lemon juice. Strain into an ice tray, cover it with foil and freeze in the ice-making compartment of the fridge (turned as low as possible) for 3 hours, stirring at hourly intervals.

Beat the egg-whites until frothy, then add the frozen syrup, a tablespoon at a time. Beat slowly until you have a dense white foam. Return it to the container, cover with foil and store in the freezer (if you have one) until needed. To make a sorbet from elder-flower wine, simply freeze one pint of the wine, then add it to the beaten egg whites as above.

Damson Ice-Cream

1 lb damsons	1 in cinnamon stick
4 oz brown sugar	½ pint single cream
2 tblsps sweet sherry	½ pint double cream
¼ pint water	

Bake the damsons, sugar, sherry, water and cinnamon in a covered dish in a low oven until soft (or use frozen or bottled damsons in this syrup – *see* page 158). Cool. Remove the cinnamon and put the damsons through the finest screen on the vegetable-mill. Whip the creams together and fold into the damson purée; sweeten, if necessary, with vanilla sugar. Pour into foil boxes, cover, and freeze, stirring occasionally, though it isn't really necessary with this ice-cream. Serve with almond biscuits.

Ginger Syllabub

2 oz ginger in syrup,
    drained and chopped
4 fl oz dry sherry
2 tblsps brandy

A litle grated nutmeg
1½ oz caster sugar
½ pint whipping cream
Ginger to decorate

Mix the sherry, brandy and nutmeg and stir in the chopped ginger. Leave to stand overnight. Next day, dissolve the sugar in the alcohol mixture. Pour in the cold cream and beat with a cold whisk (see directions on the cream tub), until thick. Spoon into small cups or bowls, decorating each with a slice of ginger. This will keep for 2-3 days in a cold larder.

Petits Pots au Fraises

1 pint milk
1 vanilla pod
3 egg yolks

1 whole egg
2 heaped tblsps vanilla sugar
8 oz sliced strawberries

Infuse the milk with the vanilla pod for about 15 minutes (the pod can then be washed, dried and stored for future use). Beat the yolks, whole egg and sugar in a basin. Remove the pod and bring the milk to just below boiling point. Pour it slowly on to the eggs and sugar, stirring all the time. Add the strawberries, and pour the mixture into little fireproof ramekins; stand them in a baking-tin of water and bake at 325° F until set (about 45-50 minutes). Chill in the fridge. You can sprinkle vanilla sugar over the top of each custard and slide them under a hot grill until the sugar caramelizes. Cool, then return to the fridge.

Any soft fruit will do for this recipe, adding more sugar to taste for raspberries.

Sweetmeat-Cream

'Take some good Cream, and slice some preserved Peaches into it, or Apricots, or Plums; sweeten the Cream with fine Sugar, or with the Syrup the Fruit was preserved in; mix these well together, and serve it cold in China Basons'. Richard Bradley, *The Country House-wife*, 1753. Try using Peaches or Apricots in brandy syrup for this (*see* pages 157-8).

SWEET DISHES

Not strictly speaking puddings or desserts, but useful to have in the larder or freezer to serve at the end of a meal.

Damson Cheese

A thick fruit paste which keeps for years and improves with keeping. Make it in a year when damsons are particularly cheap, as it needs a larger quantity of fruit than most jams and jellies.

6 lb damsons	2 whole cinnamon sticks
5-6 lb sugar	1 pint water

Wash the damsons, remove any stalks, and pack them into a large jar or casserole. Bury the cinnamon sticks amongst the fruit and add enough water to moisten the damsons. Cover the pot with foil and a lid and bake in a low oven (275° F) until the fruit is soft. Take out the cinnamon, remove the damson stones, and push the fruit through the vegetable-mill. Crack about a dozen of the damson stones and mix the kernels into the purée – they add considerably to the flavour (they do contain a certain amount of prussic acid, so don't add too many). Weigh the purée and put into a large saucepan, or preserving pan, with one pound sugar to each pound of pulp. Bring slowly to the boil, stirring often, then simmer fast for about 1¼ hours, scraping the bottom of the pan from time to time. When the mixture begins to 'candy' (i.e. look sugary) at the edges, it is ready. Pour it into shallow foil dishes, lightly greased with almond oil, and put these in a warm oven, uncovered, overnight. Next day, press disks of greaseproof paper firmly down over the surface of each cheese, then wrap the whole thing in cling-wrap. Store in a cool, dry place.

Damson cheese is very good indeed with a piece of ripe Stilton or blue Wensleydale, or you can turn it out on a plate, stick blanched almonds upright all over it and surround it with thick cream, as a dessert.

An apricot cheese can be made in the same way, using dried apricots, soaked overnight, then cooked in their soaking-water with the addition of one or two vanilla pods. Purée the fruit, weigh it and add an equal amount of sugar, and, as dried apricots now have far less flavour than formerly, add a glass or two of madeira (or a sweet sherry). Cook and store in the same way as damson cheese. Apricot cheese can be cut into neat pieces and rolled in sifted icing-sugar, to eat as sweets at Christmas.

Freezer Jams

Strawberries and raspberries lose a lot in freezing, but this method does at least preserve the flavour. It can be used in numerous ways: as fillings for sweet pancakes and cakes; sauces for steamed puddings and baked apples; and for making sorbets and ice-creams.

4 lb fresh strawberries, raspberries, or other soft fruit	2 lb caster sugar Juice 2 lemons

Mix the sugar with the whole fruit and leave it overnight in a covered bowl. Next day, put it into the blender and liquidize it. Return the purée to the bowl, stir in the strained lemon juice, then pot it in small jars (baby-food or mustard jars are perfect), leaving room for expansion as the jam freezes. To use, remove the jar from the freezer and store it in the fridge, where it will keep for about a week.

Castlegate Whitecurrant Jelly

Adapted from Eliza Acton's recipe for redcurrant jelly. It is important to remove the stalks first, as they do give the jelly a bitter taste.

2 lb whitecurrants Sugar	Large glass sweet white wine

Strip the currants with a fork – holding the bunch of currants in one hand and running the prongs of the fork down the bunch so that the currants shoot into a deep bowl. Weigh the fruit, then put it in a heavy pan with an equal quantity of sugar. Bring slowly to the boil, then boil fast for exactly 8 minutes, skimming with a perforated spoon. Tip the contents of the pan into a jelly-bag or old pillowcase and leave it to drip. Put the juice into a saucepan with the white wine, boil it up once, then pot it in warm jars. It will not set very firmly but the flavour is wonderful. This is a very good jelly to serve with *coeur à la crème* when the soft fruit season is over.

Uncooked Raspberry Jam

Their weight in sugar   Raspberries

Put the raspberries into an ovenproof dish, and the sugar into another. Put both dishes, uncovered, into a moderate oven until both sugar and raspberries are hot. Take them out, mix them rapidly and thoroughly together and pot in warm jars. This does not keep long, but has the flavour and scent of summer.

Raspberry Cream

'Take a Quart of good Cream, and put to it some Jam of Raspberries, or some Syrup of Raspberries; the Syrup will mix easiest with the Cream, but I think the Jam of Raspberries the best: You may serve this with a Desert; but if you use the Jam, you must beat it well with the Cream.' Richard Bradley, *The Country Housewife,* 1753.

Peaches or Apricots in Brandy Syrup

Ripe peaches or apricots   Sugar
Cheap grape brandy

Pour boiling water over the fruit and let it stand for 5 minutes, then remove the skins with a stainless steel knife. Halve the peaches and take out the stones, but leave apricots whole. Pack the fruit into clean jars, and fill with a syrup made from 1 lb sugar to 1½ pints water. Cover the jars and stand them in a warm oven for 1½ hours. Drain off the syrup into a measuring jug, and having measured the quantity, pour half of it off (it will make a good sorbet) and replace it with the brandy. Stir well, and pour this brandy syrup back into the jars with the warm fruit, making sure the fruit is covered. Cover tightly and store in a cool place for at least 2 months before opening.

Fruit preserved whole in brandy makes very good Christmas presents. Cut large circles from gingham or any cotton with a small pattern, and tie them over the jars with coloured tape. Label decoratively, and they will look as smart as anything from Fortnums or Jacksons, and will probably taste better (see also the recipe for olives on page 169).

Bottled Plums

Plums (Victoria, Czar,   Few cloves
   Greengage, Egg-plums or   1-2 cinnamon sticks
   Damsons)   Port, madeira or sweet sherry
Brown sugar

Wash the plums and cut a slit in each along the natural cleft in the fruit. Pack them into a stoneware jar or casserole, and for each pound of fruit add 5 oz brown sugar, 2 cloves, about 2″ cinnamon stick, ¼ pint water and a large glass of port, madeira or sherry. Cover and bake in a low oven until the fruit is soft. Transfer the fruit and syrup to warm, clean Kilner jars, filling each to the brim. Put on the metal disks but not the screw-bands, stand them in a baking-tin of hot water without touching each other and return them to a low oven (250° F) for 1½ hours. Take the jars out, stand them on a thick layer of newspaper and screw on the bands. Leave them to cool – each jar will make a loud 'pop' as the seal takes. To test for sealing, unscrew the band and try lifting the jar by the metal disk. If you can, the seal is perfect, and you can store the jar of fruit for years. Any jars which do not seal can be returned to the oven with new disks, and the process repeated. If you have a freezer, the imperfect jars can be decanted into polythene bags and frozen.

Gooseberries Bottled with Elderflowers

Gooseberries, topped, tailed
    and washed
Sugar

Water
Elderflowers, fully open

Pack clean Kilner jars with the gooseberries, and push one or two heads of elderflowers down amongst the fruit in each jar. Measure the quantity of syrup needed by pouring cold water over the fruit up to the brim of the jar, then pouring it back into a measuring jug; multiply this amount by the number of fruit-filled jars. Make a thick syrup by dissolving 12 oz sugar in each pint of water, bringing it to the boil and boiling for 5 minutes. Leave it to cool. Pour the syrup over the fruit, put on the disks, and cook as above, but as the gooseberries are raw, allow about 2½ hours cooking time. Proceed as before, placing the hot jars on thick newspaper and screwing on the bands.

Atholl Brose

Queen Victoria called this ancient Scottish recipe a 'giant's drink', and it makes a good end to a meal.

2 oz medium oatmeal
¾ pint double cream

3 tblsps clear heather honey
¼ pint whisky

Toast the oatmeal lightly under the grill. Whip the cream, stir in the honey, then fold in the oatmeal. Just before serving, add the whisky and serve in large glasses, sprinkled with a little extra toasted oatmeal.

CAKES

I must admit that although I don't really enjoy making cakes, I, and my family love eating them, especially after long walks in the country, or as an important part of a picnic.

Three Country Cakes

Parkin

This recipe has evolved over many years of parkin making, and reverses the proportions of flour to oatmeal, making a moister cake.

1 lb plain flour
½ lb medium oatmeal
6 oz brown sugar
1½ teasps ground ginger
2 teasps mixed spice
Pinch salt
2 oz mixed peel
2 oz sultanas

Just under ¾ pint water
¼ lb lard
1 lb golden syrup and
   black treacle mixed
½ teasp bicarbonate of soda
2 oz blanched split almonds
   (optional)

Mix the flour, oatmeal, sugar, spices, salt, peel and sultanas together in a large bowl. Put the water, lard and syrups into a saucepan to heat. Stand the tins of treacle without their lids in a warm oven, to make the treacle easier to pour, then judge the amount by eye – half a 1 lb tin, or a quarter of a 2 lb tin (absolute accuracy is not essential or very possible). When the lard has melted, add the bicarbonate of soda and mix well, then pour this mixture into the dry ingredients.

Mix well, stirring thoroughly. Line a roasting-tin with Bakewell paper and pour in the parkin batter. Arrange the almonds (if you are using them) in a design on the top, then bake for about 2 hours at 325° F, or until firm. Brush the top with 1 teaspoon sugar dissolved in 1 tablespoon hot water while the parkin is still warm, then let it cool in the tin. When cold, wrap it in foil and store. Don't freeze it, as it must have a chance to mature before eating. It is at its best about a week after baking.

Castlegate Fruit Cake

4 oz plain flour
4 oz wholemeal flour
1 teasp baking powder

Pinch salt
8 oz soft margarine
6 oz caster sugar

2 oz brown sugar
Grated rind and juice
  1 lemon
2 teasps mixed spice

3 large eggs
5 oz currants
5 oz sultanas
2 oz mixed peel

Cream the margarine and sugars together, with the lemon rind and spice. Beat in the eggs, one at a time, accompanying each with a spoonful of flour. Mix the rest of the flours, the baking powder, salt and the dried fruit and peel well together and fold into the creamed mixture. Add the lemon juice, and a little milk, if necessary, to make a dropping consistency. Line a large round cake tin with Bakewell paper, pour in the cake mixture and bake for 2¼ hours at 325° F, or until the cake has shrunk from the sides of the tin. Cool a little before turning onto a rack.

If you are cooking by electricity or gas, you can bake both the fruit cake and the parkin in the same oven, putting the parkin in low down and the fruit cake halfway up. As parkin is at its best about a week after baking, the fruit cake can be eaten first.

Picnic Ginger Cake

12 oz plain flour
½ teasp bicarbonate of soda
Pinch salt
8 oz soft margarine
8 oz brown sugar
Grated rind of 1 lemon

1 teasp ground ginger
2 eggs (well beaten)
12 oz golden syrup
4 oz sultanas
Lemon icing (*see recipe*)

Cream the margarine and sugar, with the lemon rind and ginger. Warm the syrup in a saucepan, beat the eggs into the creamed mixture, then add the syrup, gradually. Mix the soda well with the flour, then stir in the sultanas, and fold all into the cake mixture. Bake in a Bakewell lined cake tin for 1½ hours at 325° F. Cool a little, remove from the tin and leave the cake to get quite cold before icing. Sift 4 oz icing sugar into a bowl and stir in enough lemon juice to make a stiffish pouring consistency. Spread this over the cake, allowing some of the icing to dribble down the sides.

Three Elegant Cakes

Austrian Chocolate Cake

3 oz good plain chocolate
4 oz unsalted butter
4 oz vanilla sugar
Pinch mixed spice
Few drops almond essence

Grated rind of 1 orange
2 eggs
2 oz plain flour
½ teasp baking powder
4 oz ground almonds

Covering :

2 oz plain chocolate

4 tblsps bitter marmalade

Grease and flour a cake tin with a removeable base. Heat the oven to 350° F. Break the chocolate into pieces and put it to melt in a basin over hot water. Beat the butter, sugar, spice, almond essence and orange rind together until light, then beat in the eggs, one at a time, and the melted chocolate. Beat hard for at least a minute. Mix the flour, baking powder and ground almonds together and fold them into the cake mixture quickly and lightly. Pour into the prepared tin and bake for about 1 hour, or until the mixture has shrunk a little from the sides of the tin. Cool a little before turning it out on to a wire rack. To store, wrap it in a couple of layers of cling-wrap. It will be all the better if kept a day or two before eating. Glaze the cake with the marmalade, then grate the chocolate over the top, using the coarse part of the grater. With lots of whipped cream, it makes an excellent dessert.

Rich Coffee Cake

2 tblsps good instant coffee
1 tblsp hot water
4 oz soft margarine
6 oz caster sugar
1 egg

¼ pint sour cream
8 oz plain flour
1 teasp baking powder
½ teasp bicarbonate of soda

Dissolve the coffee in the hot water, and add it to the creamed sugar and margarine. Beat in the egg, then add the sour cream, and finally fold in the flour mixed with the baking powder and soda. Bake in a greased cake tin, dusted with flour, for about 1 hour at 350° F. Cool on a rack. Split in half and fill with chocolate butter icing made as follows: Cream 4 oz unsalted butter with 4 oz sifted icing sugar. Dissolve 3 teasps cocoa in 1 tblsp hot water and blend with the butter and icing sugar until light. Ice the top of the cake with 3 oz icing sugar and 1 oz cocoa sifted together, and a knob of butter and a little hot water beaten in to give a glossy spreading consistency. This is a very good adult birthday cake, as it is not too sweet.

Walnut Cake

8 oz plain flour	4 oz chopped walnuts
2½ teasps baking powder	4 fl oz milk
3 oz butter	Apricot jam
8 oz vanilla sugar	Glacé icing
2 eggs, yolks and whites separated	Walnut halves

Sift together the flour and baking powder. Cream the butter and sugar until fluffy, then beat in the egg yolks and chopped walnuts. Fold in the flour, adding it alternately with the milk (which should be at room temperature, not straight out of the fridge). Then add the stiffly beaten egg-whites. Pour the mixture into a greased and floured cake tin and bake for 35 minutes at 375° F. Cool, split the cake and sandwich it with plenty of apricot jam. Cover the top with 4 oz icing sugar moistened to a spreading consistency with warm water, then decorate with the walnut halves.

Finally, a tea-bread or yeast cake from Italy. It makes a delicious bread-and-butter pudding, should you have any left over, with the addition of 2 tablespoons sweet sherry or marsala to the egg and milk custard.

Pandolce

12 oz plain flour	2 oz vanilla sugar
½ teasp cinnamon	¼ teasp grated nutmeg
Pinch salt	Grated rind of 1 orange

Mix these ingredients together, rubbing in the orange peel so that it is evenly distributed. Cover the bowl and leave it in a warm place.

½ tblsp dried yeast   Pinch sugar
4 tblsps lukewarm water

Whisk the yeast and sugar into the water with a fork and leave for
10-15 minutes by the stove until the yeast looks like Guinness froth.
Make a well in the middle of the warmed dry ingredients and pour
into it:

The frothy yeast   2 lightly beaten eggs
2 oz butter, melted in   1 tblsp triple orange
2 tblsps warm milk   flower water

Bring in the flour, working first of all with a wooden spoon, then
with your hands, until you have a lithe and springy ball of dough
which leaves the bowl clean. If the eggs were large, and the dough
sticky, add sprinkles of flour until you have the right consistency.
Cut a deep cross in the ball of dough, cover it with a cloth and leave
it to rise in a warm place for about 1 hour. Meanwhile:

Soak 2 oz sultanas in 2 tblsps triple orange flower water

When the dough has risen, drain the sultanas and mix them with

1 oz chopped almonds   1 oz mixed peel

and knead into the dough; try to distribute the fruit and nuts evenly
throughout the dough. Form it into a thick roll and either fit it
into a greased ring mould, or make it into a circle by joining the
two ends together. Put it on a floured baking sheet and leave it to
prove while the oven heats to 400° F. Bake for 40 minutes, then
take it out and tap it on the bottom with your knuckles – if it sounds
hollow it is done – if not, return it upside down to the oven for
another 10 minutes. As the *pandolce* cools on a cake rack, brush
the top with 2 tablespoons sugar dissolves in 1 tablespoon hot water.
This is a great treat for breakfast, spread with butter.

BISCUITS

Biscuits are lovely to make when you have plenty of time – on a
wet Saturday afternoon, when there are children who can help with
the rolling, cutting and filling. The first recipe is child's play: my
daughter's school recipe for a very good cheap shortbread.

Lucy's Shortbread

5 oz plain flour	2 oz caster sugar
1 oz cornflour	4 oz soft margarine

Mix the dry ingredients together, then work in the margarine until you have a ball of stiff dough. Press it out flat with the heel of your hand in a greased 7 in flan tin, prick it all over with a fork and mark into sections with a knife. Cook at 300° F. until pale gold – about 35 minutes – 'and hope that it will come out right'. It usually does.

Royal Biscuits

Originally from the Aga cookery book, this is a recipe for Imperial Biscuits, requiring three different jams. My mother quickly adapted it to a more labour-saving version, using only one kind of jam (black-currant and plum are best), though that should be home-made.

4 oz sugar	½ teasp baking powder
4 oz butter	Pinch salt
1 egg	1 teasp ground cinnamon
8 oz flour	Jam (see above)

Cream the butter and sugar together until light; mix in the beaten egg, then the flour sifted with the baking powder, salt and cinnamon. Knead until smooth, turn on to a floured board and roll out thinly. Cut into circles, and from the centres of half of them remove a smaller circle (an apple-corer will do this). Bake the biscuits on a greased baking sheet for about 15 minutes in a moderate oven (350° F). Cool on a wire rack. When cold, spread jam on the whole biscuits, dredge the holed ones thickly with icing sugar and sand-wich the two together.

Almond Biscuits

For serving with syllabubs, ice-creams, sorbets and custards.

4 oz butter	2 oz chopped almonds
7 oz caster sugar	8 oz plain flour
1 egg	2 teasps baking powder
1 teasp almond essence	Pinch salt

Cream the butter and sugar, beat in the egg and almond essence, then the almonds. Sift the flour with the salt and baking powder and mix it in quickly and lightly to form a soft dough. Shape it into a roll about 2″ in diameter, wrap it in foil and keep in the fridge until needed. To bake the biscuits, heat the oven to 375° F, shave off portions of the dough with a sharp knife and bake them on a baking sheet for 10 minutes. The dough will keep for some time, and is very useful when you have a lot of people to feed.

Tollhouse Cookies

One of the best of the many good American biscuit recipes.

3½ oz butter	3 oz chopped nuts
6 tblsps granulated sugar	6 oz chocolate pieces
6 tblsps brown sugar	6 oz plain flour
½ teasp vanilla essence	½ teasp baking powder
1 egg	½ teasp salt

Cream together the butter and sugars, together with the essence. Beat in the egg, the nuts and chocolate pieces. Sift together the flour, baking powder and salt and mix in thoroughly. Drop teaspoons of this mixture (adding a little milk if it is too stiff) fairly far apart on greased baking sheets. Cook for 10-12 minutes at 375° F. Remove the biscuits from the baking sheets while still warm and cool on a wire rack.

Bridget's Flapjacks

Much more interesting than the ordinary kind.

12 oz porridge oats	8 oz butter
½ teasp salt	4 tblsps golden syrup
1 oz sunflower seeds	4 oz soft brown sugar
2 oz bran	
1 oz flaked almonds and sesame seeds, mixed	

Mix all the dry ingredients together except the sugar. Put the sugar in a pan with the butter and syrup and heat gently until the butter has melted. Stir this into the dry ingredients. Spread evenly into a greased swiss-roll tin and bake at 350° F for about 25 minutes, or until crisp on top. Mark into squares with a knife while still warm, then cool a little in the tin before putting the flapjacks on a wire tray.

Christmas Spice Biscuits

These look very pretty hung on the Christmas tree, but they will go soft, so keep some in an airtight tin for eating.

2 oz soft brown sugar	½ teasp each ground ginger,
2 oz lard	cloves, nutmeg, cinnamon
½ large tea-cup black treacle	and allspice
9 oz plain flour	½ teasp baking powder

Put the sugar, lard and treacle in a saucepan and heat gently until the lard melts. Mix together all the other ingredients, making sure all the spices are well blended into the flour. Pour the lard and treacle into the flour and stir well; then use your hands to make a stiff dough. Refrigerate it for half an hour, then roll it out very thinly – cut it into suitable shapes – stars, hearts, etc. Make a small hole near the top of some with a skewer. Arrange the biscuits on a greased baking sheet (they won't spread, so you can put them close together) and cook for 8-10 minutes at 375° F. Cool and decorate with white icing (left from icing the cake, perhaps); thread red wool or cotton through the biscuits with holes and hang them on the tree. Store the others carefully. This dough keeps for months in the fridge, so you can prepare it well in advance.

Miscellaneous
Ideas&
Recipes

Miscellaneous Ideas and Recipes

Olives in Oil

These make very good presents and are a useful way of storing olives with benefit both to the olives and the oil.

Best quality black and green olives – buy them loose from a really good Soho delicatessen, or try the vacuum-packed ones by Barral

Good olive oil
Sprigs of fresh thyme, rosemary
Bayleaves
Whole, peeled, cloves garlic

Put the olives into screw-top jars with the garlic and herbs, and top-up the jars with olive oil. If you are doing this for yourself, rather than for presents, you can improve an indifferent make of olive oil by this method, rather than use a good one in the first place. The quantity of herbs used depends on your taste, but don't use too much garlic.

Pickled Jerusalem Artichokes

These can form part of any mixed *hors d'oeuvre* and are particularly good when eaten with the olives above. Thinly sliced, they add variety to a potato salad.

3 sprigs thyme
4 whole cloves garlic
4 peppercorns

2 lb Jerusalem artichokes
White wine vinegar
3 bayleaves

Scrub the artichokes, then boil them for 10 minutes in salted water – they should be underdone. When they are cool enough to handle, peel and slice them, and put them into clean jars. Measure the amount of vinegar you will need by filling one of the jars with vinegar, draining it off into a measuring jug and multiplying this amount by the number of filled jars. Put the vinegar in a pan, add the herbs, garlic and peppercorns and put over a low heat for half-an-hour for the flavours to infuse. Cool the vinegar before pouring it over the artichokes, and add the flavouring herbs to the jars, to add to the appearance as well as to the flavour. Keep for at least a month before using.

Pickled Damsons

Very good with any cold meat, but particularly cold salt pork.

3 lb damsons	1½ lb brown sugar
½ pint red wine vinegar	6 cloves
Cinnamon stick,	
broken into short pieces	

Prick the damsons all over with a skewer or carving-fork. Put them in a large saucepan with all the ingredients and bring slowly to the boil. Once they have boiled, lift the damsons out of the syrup with a perforated spoon and put them in a bowl, leaving the syrup to simmer for another 10 minutes; pour it over the damsons and leave them overnight. Next day reboil the fruit for a minute, lift it out of the syrup and continue to boil that for another 10 minutes. Leave for another 24 hours, then repeat the process. This time, pot both damsons and syrup (strain it of the spices if you like) in warm jars. Use plastic lids or jam covers as vinegar will corrode metal lids. Keep for 2 months before using.

Spiced Oranges

Delicious with roast pork and duck, and beautiful to look at.

¾ pint white wine vinegar	2 lb sugar
½ nutmeg – ungrated	6 large juicy oranges
6 cloves	About ½ pint water
Cinnamon stick	

Put the vinegar, spices and sugar into a pan and boil for about 10 minutes. Slice the unpeeled oranges fairly thickly and put them into another saucepan with just enough water to cover them. Simmer gently until the peel is tender. Drain and reserve the liquor. Put the orange slices into the pan with the vinegar syrup (if there is not enough to cover them, add some of the reserved liquor) and cook gently for about half-an-hour, or until the slices become transparent. Put both oranges and syrup into a bowl and leave overnight. Next day, drain the slices and put them in a large jar (try to fit them into one large jar, rather than using several small ones). Reboil the syrup until thick, let it cool a little, strain it of the spices and pour it over the oranges. Cover tightly and keep for at least 2-3 months before using.

Dried Apricot Chutney

1 lb cooking apples, peeled, cored and chopped

½ lb dried apricots, soaked overnight

4 whole cloves garlic, peeled

1 large chopped onion

Rind and juice of 1 lemon, cut the rind into strips

Rind and juice of 1 orange, cut the rind into strips

2 teasps salt

1 oz pickling spices tied in an old handkerchief

1 pint cider vinegar

4 oz sultanas

1 lb brown sugar

Put all the ingredients except the sugar, into a large pan and cook very slowly until all is soft. Add the sugar, stir well, bring to the boil and simmer until thick – about 20 minutes. Remove the bag of spices, pot the chutney and cover tightly. It is ready for use immediately, and does not keep very well; it can be made at any time of year, however, using eating apples if no cookers are available.

Brandy Butter

Less sweet than usual recipes which call for twice as much sugar as butter.

8 oz unsalted butter

4 oz soft brown sugar, or caster sugar

3 tblsps brandy

Grated rind and juice of 1 lemon

Freshly ground coriander

Cut the butter into pieces and melt it slowly in a saucepan. Stir in all the other ingredients. Put the saucepan in a cold larder, or in the fridge, and stir from time to time as the butter cools. Pot, when cold, in stoneware jars with lids.

Roast Lemons

'For a Cough. Roast a large Lemon very carefully without burning; when it is thorough hot, cut and squeeze it into a Cup, upon three Ounces of Sugar-candy finely powdered; take a Spoonful whenever your Cough troubles you.'

Daily Bread

Makes 2 loaves

12 oz strong plain flour	½ tblsp dried yeast
12 oz coarse wholemeal flour	Just under ¾ pint
Generous ½ oz salt	luke-warm water
¼ teasp sugar	

Stir the yeast and sugar into the water and put it in a warm place for 10-15 minutes – until frothy. Mix the flours and salt and make a well in the middle. Pour in the yeast and water and mix until you have a springy dough. Knead for a minute or two. Shape it into a ball, put it in a floured bowl, cut a cross through it, cover with a cloth and leave in a warm place until double in size (about 2 hours). Knead again. Shape into two slightly rounded balls, cut a shallow cross on each and put on a greased baking sheet. Cover and leave to prove for 30 minutes. Heat the oven to 425° F, put in the bread and lower the heat to 350° F after 10 minutes. Bake for another 30 minutes. Remove from the oven and tap the bottom of the loaves; if they sound hollow they are ready, if not, replace them upside down in the oven for a further 5-10 minutes.

Crumble Mixture

To store in the fridge. With bottled fruit it makes a better instant pudding than anything out of a packet.

1 lb plain flour	8 oz unsalted butter
½ teasp mixed spice	8 oz demerara sugar

Rub the butter into the flour and spice until fine, then mix in the sugar. Store in a plastic tub with a well fitting lid.

Garlic and Herb Cheese

4 oz fresh cream cheese	½ clove garlic,
1 tblsp chopped fresh herbs,	finely chopped
according to season	Pinch salt

Mix the cheese thoroughly with the herbs and garlic, then taste to check seasoning. Put into a small pot with a lid and store in the fridge (wrap the whole jar in foil or everything else will taste of garlic).

Preliminary Preparation of Dried Beans and Peas

I find this method very useful, as it doesn't need quite as much fore-thought as the ordinary preparation by soaking. Also, in warm weather soaking pulses start to ferment more quickly than you realize.

Weigh the beans first, according to how many you need for the recipe, wash them and put them into a pan with a tightly fitting lid. Add a pinch of bicarbonate of soda to help soften them (but no salt, which makes them hard), and enough cold water to cover them by a good two inches. Bring slowly to the boil, take them off the heat and leave them, without removing the lid, for 45 minutes. Drain the beans and continue according to the recipe.

Butter Papers

These are so useful that it is criminal to throw them away. Keep them in a polythene box or bag in the fridge and use them to grease baking tins, cover casseroles during long cooking, baste poultry, grease frying-pans when only the smallest amount of fat is needed for, say, pancakes, and even to smooth sledge runners and skate blades.

Herbs & Spices

Herbs and Spices - a quick guide

Basil An annual which needs warmth and plenty of sun. Use it for tomato dishes, and sparingly with eggs. Basil vinegar is made by putting a large sprig in a bottle of red wine vinegar and is very good for enlivening winter stews.

Bay-leaves A charming small tree for growing in a tub – bring it in for the winter in cold areas. A vital ingredient of *bouquets garnis*.

Bergamot A very decorative herbaceous plant with shaggy red flowers which make a good addition to a plain green salad. Bees like it, and the leaves make a fragrant tea. It prefers light shade.

Borage The blue flowers of this herb are an important ingredient of Pimms, and wine cups generally. It can take over the garden, so plant with care. The leaves have a faint flavour of cucumbers.

Celery Celery leaves are a frequently forgotten but extremely useful winter flavouring; a good ingredient for *bouquets garnis*, and for adding, chopped, to ordinary mashed potatoes.

Chervil Easily grown, as it will seed itself with gusto. Its mild aniseed flavour combines well with chives and parsley in herb mixtures for omelettes, butters, sauces, etc. It loses its delicate flavour if cooked for long.

Chives Their mild onion flavour is compatible with most things; use them to flavour cream cheese, potato dishes, salads, mayonnaise. The purple flowers are very pretty.

Elder This beautiful shrub grows wild and is often uprooted as a weed, which is a pity, as the flowers given a delicious muscatel flavour to syrups and sorbets, and make a good wine. The berries are good in fruit salads and apple pies.

Fennel A handsome plant with feathery leaves and aromatic stalks which can be used when smoking fish. Use sparingly in sauces to serve with fish. Italian fennel (which has white onion-like bulb) is very difficult to grow in this country, despite what seed catalogues might tell you.

Juniper Buy the berries to flavour game, pork and veal dishes. It can be grown in the garden, but will take many years to produce berries.

Marjoram A neat plant which can be grown in pots as well as in the garden. Goes well with all meat, especially lamb.

Mint This spreads fast, so plant it inside some sort of root restrictor, such as an old drain-pipe. Use it to flavour cucumber salads, as well as to cook with new potatoes. Eau-de-cologne mint is useful for pot-pourri.

Parsley Temperamental in some gardens (dislikes acid soil), but can be bought fresh and kept in a polythene box in the fridge. Very good when finely chopped with garlic and used with shellfish and chicken. Also good in dumplings, forcemeat balls, stuffings, and sprinkled on soups and stews.

Rosemary An aromatic evergreen shrub with small flowers of a beautiful blue, enjoyed by bees. Grows well in a sheltered spot on poorish soil. Particularly good with pork and chicken. Dries well.

Sage A favourite English herb, but it should be used *very* sparingly; can be used to flavour pork and poultry. 'Red' sage is an attractive variety for the herb garden.

Sorrel Can be grown in the garden, but is very easy to find growing wild. It likes damp long grass, and its narrow, shiny dark green leaves have a refreshing acid taste. Use as a filling for omelettes, and make a sauce for serving with veal, chicken, young lamb and mackerel. Does not dry well, but can be frozen.

Tarragon Buy the 'true French' variety for the best flavour, and grow it in a pot, as it is tender in many areas. The best of all herbs for chicken and fish. Unlike chervil, its delicate aniseed flavour does not disappear with cooking. Tarragon vinegar can be made by putting a large piece in a bottle of white wine vinegar.

Thyme Many varieties are decorative rather than culinary. Use common thyme for flavouring stuffings, and lemon thyme for fish. A sprig of thyme used to flavour gravy for roast beef or game makes a good change.

SPICES Buy whole spices whenever possible, as once powdered they quickly lose their pungency. Indian spices are best bought from Indian grocers, as they will probably be fresher.

Allspice Like large peppercorns, allspice can be used with pepper to give extra aroma in all meat dishes, especially game, and in pâtés.

Caraway Pungent seeds used in English cookery to flavour cakes and sweet dishes. Also good with cabbage, beetroot, carrot salad, and to make soup (see recipe on page 38).

Cardamom Small black very aromatic seeds housed in an outer husk. Crush them lightly and add to Middle Eastern and Indian dishes.

Cayenne Very fiery pepper best bought in small quantities, as it doesn't keep well. Use it for cheese and fish dishes.

Cinnamon Buy the whole sticks for flavouring syrups, mulled wine, game casseroles, and powdered for cakes, etc.

Cloves Buy these whole to use for seasoning onion and bread sauces, stocks, soups and stews. Use powdered cloves for cakes. Be sparing – too many cloves ruin an apple pie.

Coriander Always buy the whole seeds, and keep a special grinder for them. Use them for all sorts of dishes which will benefit from their warm orange flavour – pork, duck, lamb.

Cumin Indian spice with seeds rather like caraway seeds. Use it whole or powdered in pilaffs and curries.

Ginger Dried ginger root can be grated on a nutmeg grater for use in cakes and puddings. Fresh 'green' ginger root can be peeled and stored, covered with sherry, in a screw-top jar in the fridge. Add small pieces to curries, and other Indian dishes; the sherry makes a delicious syllabub.

Mace The golden filigree husk of the nutmeg, its flavour is similar, but milder. Use the whole 'blades' to infuse in sauces or stocks, and in powdered form for cakes.

Nutmeg Buy whole nutmegs and a grater with a compartment at the back to hold the nut. Use it freshly grated to season Italian meat sauces and stews, pâtés and cheese dishes, and sweet dishes such as custards, also to flavour hot drinks and vegetables.

Paprika Ask for *edel-süss* ('noble-sweet') paprika in delicatessens for the best flavour, and use it to season goulashes and veal dishes generally. Also good sprinkled on cabbage.

Pepper Always use this freshly ground – the white peppercorns for strength and the black for flavour. Try mixing the two (one-third white to two-thirds black) in your pepper-mill. Green peppercorns are widely available now and have a uniquely aromatic pungency which goes well with game, lamb, pork, chicken and fish. They are sold in brine; drain and crush them before using.

Saffron Extremely expensive but worth it, for giving rice an aromatic flavour and beautiful golden colour for serving as part of a paella, or with Mediterranean tomato-based stews of meat and fish.

Salt Use ordinary cooking salt, or block salt in the kitchen, and keep Maldon salt crystals or sea-salt for the table, where their flavour is best appreciated.

Turmeric Can be used as a cheaper alternative to saffron, but is delicious in its own right. Use it for Middle Eastern and Indian dishes.

Vanilla One of the most important flavourings in the kitchen. Avoid the essence, which often gives a synthetic flavour if used too generously, and use the pods. Keep two or three in a large jar of caster sugar for flavouring cakes and puddings, and infuse the pods in syrups and custards. They can be washed, dried and re-used.

Comparative Weights and Measures

SOLID MEASURES

English	Metric
2 lb 3 oz	1 kilogram (1000 grammes)
1 lb $1\frac{1}{2}$ oz	500 gr
9 oz	250 gr
$4\frac{1}{4}$ oz	125 gr
$3\frac{1}{2}$ oz	100 gr

LIQUID MEASURES

$1\frac{3}{4}$ pints (35 fl oz)	1 litre
just over $\frac{3}{4}$ pint ($17\frac{1}{2}$ fl oz)	$\frac{1}{2}$ litre
just under $\frac{1}{2}$ pint ($8\frac{3}{4}$ fl oz)	$\frac{1}{4}$ litre
about 3 fl oz	1 decilitre
about 1 dessertspoon	1 centilitre

OVEN TEMPERATURES

Gas		Electricity	
		°C	°F
$\frac{1}{2}$	Very slow	120	250
1	Slow	140	275
2		150	300
3	Warm	160	325
4	Moderate	180	350
5	Fairly hot	190	375
6	Hot	200	400
7		220	425
8	Very hot	230	450
9		240	475
10		250	500

Bibliography

MEAT PRESERVATION

Meat Preserving at Home, Maggie Black (London, EP Publishing Ltd, 1976).

Charcuterie and French Pork Cookery, Jane Grigson (Penguin, 1970).

GARDENING

The Vegetable Book, Terence Conran and Maria Kroll (London, Collins (William), Sons & Co Ltd, 1976).

Indoor Farming, David Wickers (London, Julian Friedmann Publishers Ltd, 1977).

In a Herb Garden, George Jones (Venton Educational, 1977).

Catalogue from Scotts Nurseries, Merriott, Somerset

GENERAL INTEREST

The Country Housewife, Richard Bradley (1753).

The Experienced English Housekeeper, Elizabeth Raffald (1794).

Modern Cookery, Eliza Acton (Longmans Green, 1855 edition; first published 1845).

A Book of Middle Eastern Food, Claudia Roden (Penguin, 1970).

The Scots Kitchen, F. Marian McNeill (London, Mayflower Books Ltd, 1974).

All books by Jane Grigson and Elizabeth David, particularly Mrs Grigson's *English Food* and Mrs David's *French Provincial Cooking*.

Index